CLEAN BREAK

Clean Break in association with Soho Theatre presents

CHARGED

Writers	**E V Crowe**
	Sam Holcroft
	Rebecca Lenkiewicz
	Chloë Moss
	Winsome Pinnock
	Rebecca Prichard
Directors	**Lucy Morrison**
	Caroline Steinbeis
	Tessa Walker
Designer	**Soutra Gilmour**
Lighting Designer	**Johanna Town**
Sound Designer	**Emma Laxton**
Costume Supervisor	**Sian Harris**
Production Manager	**Bo Barton**

Charged was commissioned by
Clean Break's Head of Artistic Programme Lucy Morrison

10–27 November 2010
Soho Theatre, London
Box Office 020 7478 0100
www.sohotheatre.com
BSL-interpreted performances 23 and 25 November

The six plays in **Charged** were performed in two cycles of three plays each.
'Charged 1' comprises: **Dream Pill** by Rebecca Prichard, **Fatal Light**
by Chloë Moss, **Taken** by Winsome Pinnock
'Charged 2' comprises: **Dancing Bears** by Sam Holcroft, **That Almost
Unnameable Lust** by Rebecca Lenkiewicz, **Doris Day** by E V Crowe

Dream Pill by Rebecca Prichard

Cast

BOLA	**Danielle Vitalis**
TUNDE	**Samantha Pearl**

Production Team

Director	**Tessa Walker**
Stage Manager	**Sarah Tryfan**
Assistant Stage Manager	**Chloe R Brown**

Fatal Light by Chloë Moss

Cast

AINE	**Isabella Mason**
JAY	**Rebecca Scroggs**
KERRY	**Ony Uhiara**
MAGGIE	**Ashley McGuire**
POLICEWOMAN	**Emma Noakes**

Production Team

Director and Dramaturg	**Lucy Morrison**
Stage Manager	**Claire Essex**
Assistant Stage Manager	**Teya Lanzon**

Taken by Winsome Pinnock

Cast

DELLA	**Beatie Edney**
NANA NOLA	**Janet Henfrey**
NOLA	**Rebecca Oldfield**

Production Team

Director	**Caroline Steinbeis**
Stage Manager	**Rebecca Carnell**
Assistant Stage Manager	**Dayna Moyes**

Dancing Bears by Sam Holcroft

Cast

AARON	**Emmanuella Cole**
ANGRY / BABYMOTHER	**Danielle Vitalis**
DEAN / RAZOR KAY	**Ony Uhiara**
RETARD / CHARITY	**Samantha Pearl**

Production Team

Director	**Tessa Walker**
Stage Manager	**Sarah Tryfan**
Assistant Stage Manager	**Chloe R Brown**

That Almost Unnameable Lust by Rebecca Lenkiewicz

Cast

KATHERINE	**Janet Henfrey**
LIZ	**Beatie Edney**
WRITER	**Rebecca Oldfield**

Production Team

Director	**Caroline Steinbeis**
Stage Manager	**Rebecca Carnell**
Assistant Stage Manager	**Dayna Moyes**

Doris Day by E V Crowe

Cast

ANNA	**Rebecca Scroggs**
DAISY	**Emma Noakes**

Production Team

Director	**Lucy Morrison**
Stage Manager	**Claire Essex**
Assistant Stage Manager	**Teya Lanzon**

Foreword

Charged is an epic moment for Clean Break. A moment when thirty-one years of making theatre and delivering theatre education with thousands of women come together through six new and powerful stories. These stories reveal the damage meted out by neglectful families, abusive partners, the criminal justice system and a society that too often turns away and shuns these women. Labelled as offenders, prisoners, inmates, criminals and failures, they are also mothers, sisters, daughters, grandmothers, friends and lovers. *Charged* is a celebration of these women's courage, dignity, strength and endurance.

Charged is also a celebration of women as theatre artists. This production brings together, for the first time, six extraordinary women playwrights. Four come from a long line of writers that have been commissioned by the company: Chloë Moss (*This Wide Night*), E V Crowe (*A Just Act*), Winsome Pinnock (*Mules*) and Rebecca Prichard (*Yard Gal*). Two – Rebecca Lenkiewicz and Sam Holcroft – are new to Clean Break. Each playwright chose her own theme, met with women offenders and criminal justice practitioners as part of the research process, and wrote their individual contributions to *Charged*. Clean Break then matched these writers with three gifted directors – Lucy Morrison, Caroline Steinbeis and Tessa Walker – and employed a skilled team of thirty more women theatre practitioners. In a male-dominated sector, employment for women in theatre is certainly alive and kicking at Clean Break. They are the writers, the directors, the stage managers and the creatives behind the scenes. They are the actors – of ages spanning eight decades in *Charged*. And they are the workshop leaders, the administrators and the producers that make these plays possible.

We hope that the 2010 Soho Theatre production of *Charged* will be but the beginning of its journey, reaching more audiences in theatres, women's centres and prisons. We hope that, wherever it is seen, it will be followed by conversation, discovery, determination and hope. We would like to thank everyone who has worked so hard to make this ambitious production possible, with particular thanks to the writers, directors and *Charged* teams, the Clean Break staff team, Soho Theatre for another successful partnership, the Network for Social Change and Arts Council England. Finally, we dedicate these plays to the women for whom our company was founded.

Lucy Perman MBE
Executive Director
Clean Break

Cast, Creative and Production Team

Bo Barton
(Production Manager)
Bo worked for many years as a freelance Stage, Company and Production Manager before spending seven years as Production Manager at the Royal Court Theatre. For the following seven years she was Director of Technical Training at RADA, before returning to freelance work. Companies she has worked with include: Shared Experience, English Touring Theatre, MJE Productions, Lyric Hammersmith, Grange Park Opera, and Northampton Theatres Trust.

Chloe R Brown
(Assistant Stage Manager, *Dancing Bears* and *Dream Pill*)
Chloe is currently in her final year of study on the Stage Management course at Rose Bruford College. Recent work includes: *Dr Faustus* (Unicorn); *A Little Night Music* (Royal Academy of Music). She also holds the role of Company Stage Manager for Freshcut Productions, a theatre company created with fellow students from Rose Bruford College. Freshcut Productions produced *You're a Good Man, Charlie Brown* as part of the Camden Fringe (2010).

Rebecca Carnell
(Stage Manager, *Taken* and *That Almost Unnameable Lust*)
Rebecca trained at the Bristol Old Vic Theatre School. Recent work includes: *The Lady from the Sea*, *She Stoops to Conquer* (Birmingham Rep); *Ten Tiny Toes* (Liverpool Everyman); *The Pillowman*, *The Lieutenant of Inishmore* (Curve, Leicester); *La bohème* (Opera Holland Park); *Another Door Closed* (Bath Theatre Royal); *Mrs Warren's Profession* (as Deputy Stage Manager, Comedy); *it felt empty when the heart went at first but it is alright now* (as Deputy Stage Manager, Clean Break).

Emmanuella Cole
(AARON, *Dancing Bears*)
Emmanuella trained at the Central School of Speech and Drama. Theatre includes: *Danton's Death* (NT); *African Snow* (Trafalgar Studios/national tour); *This Wide Night* (Bernie Grant Art Centre); *Silverland* (Arcola). Television includes: *Thorne: Sleepyhead*, *Little Miss Jocelyn*, *EastEnders*.

E V Crowe
(Writer, *Doris Day*)
E V Crowe has an MA in Creative Writing from the University of East Anglia. She was a member of the Royal Court Theatre Young Writers Programme in 2005, and the Royal Court's 'Super Group 2009'. She has been on attachment to the Royal Court (2007), and the National Theatre Studio (2010). Her previous work includes: *A Just Act* (Clean Break, 2009); *Number 1*, *Community Hall* (Bush, Wraparound Response and Election short); *One Runs the Other Doesn't* (Royal Court Rough Cuts, 2010). Autumn 2010 productions include: *Kin* (Royal Court); *ROTOR* (Siobhan Davies Dance Studios).

Beatie Edney
(DELLA, *Taken* and LIZ, *That Almost Unnameable Lust*)
Theatre includes: *Alice* (Sheffield Crucible); *The Girlfriend Experience* (Royal Court/Young Vic); *Dead Funny*, *Tango at the End of Winter*, *Les Liaisons Dangereuses* (West End/Broadway); *Summer Begins* (Donmar

Warehouse). Television includes: *Law & Order UK*, *Poirot: The Clocks*, *Wallander*, *New Tricks*, *Kenneth Williams*, *Fantabulosa!*, *Messiah*, *The Tenant of Wildfell Hall*, *Prime Suspect 4*, *The Dark Angel*, *Inspector Morse*, *Lost Empires*, *Dressing for Breakfast*. Film includes: *In the Name of the Father*, *Mister Johnson*, *A Handful of Dust*, *Highlander*.

Claire Essex
(Stage Manager, *Doris Day* and *Fatal Light*)
Claire has been working professionally as a Stage Manager since graduating from the Bristol Old Vic Theatre School in 2006. Recent productions include: *Scorched* (Old Vic Tunnels); *The Glass Menagerie* (Shared Experience/UK tour); *The Love of Three Oranges* (Grange Park Opera). Claire also worked extensively with Salisbury Playhouse for three years and worked for two seasons with the Open Air Theatre, Regent's Park.

Renee Ge
(Assistant Stage Manager, *Charged*)
Renee has been associated with Clean Break since 2008. She has worked on two Clean Break productions, *it felt empty when the heart went at first but it is alright now* (Arcola, 2009), and the reprisal of *This Wide Night* (Soho, 2009). She has also been involved in three Clean Break education programme productions, including the Performance Level 1 play *Soft Scoop* (2010) and the Access to Community Theatre final productions *The Boiler Room* (2009) and *She from the Sea* (LIFT Festival, 2010).

Soutra Gilmour
(Designer)
Theatre work includes: *Bedlam* (Shakespeare's Globe); *Into the Woods* (Open Air Theatre, Regent's Park); *Salome* (Headlong, Hampstead); *Polar Bears* (Donmar Warehouse); *The Little Dog Laughed* (Garrick); *Three Days of Rain* (Apollo); *The Pride* (Royal Court); *The Tragedy of Thomas Hobbes* (RSC at Wilton's Music Hall); *Piaf* (Donmar Warehouse/Vaudeville/Teatro Liceo, Buenos Aires); *The Lover & The Collection* (Comedy); *Our Friends in the North*, *Ruby Moon*, *Son of Man* (Northern Stage); *Last Easter* (Birmingham Rep); *Angels in America* (Headlong, Lyric Hammersmith); *Bad Jazz*, *A Brief History of Helen of Troy* (ATC); *The Birthday Party* (Sheffield Crucible); *The Caretaker* (Sheffield Crucible/Tricycle); *Petrol Jesus Nightmare #5 (in the Time of the Messiah)* (Traverse/Kosovo); *Lovers & War* (Strindberg's Intima Theatre, Stockholm); *Hair*, *Witness* (Gate); *Baby Doll*, *Thérèse Raquin* (Citizens, Glasgow); *Ghost City* (59E59, New York); *When Tte World Was Green* (Young Vic); *Modern Dance for Beginners* (Soho); *Shadow of a Boy* (NT).

Sian Harris
(Costume Supervisor)
Sian trained in fashion but has worked in the theatre for over twenty years. Recent work includes: *Pelléas and Mélisande*, *Don Giovanni* (Opera Holland Park); *Dunsinane* (RSC); *Bingo*, *Wallenstein* (Chichester Festival Theatre); *Dallas Sweetman* (Paines Plough, Canterbury Cathedral); *The Magic Flute*, *A Night at the Chinese Opera*, *The Marriage of Figaro*, *Albert Herring* (Royal Academy of Music); *Hurts Given and Received*, *Slowly* (The Wrestling School); *Wozzeck* (Philharmonia Orchestra); *The History of Dr Johann Faustus* (London Philharmonic Orchestra); *La bohème* (British Youth Opera).

Janet Henfrey
(NANA NOLA in *Taken* and KATHERINE in *That Almost Unnameable Lust*)
Theatre includes: *All's Well That Ends Well, The Good Person of Sichuan*
(NT); *The Merry Wives of Windsor, Pericles, The Two Gentlemen of
Verona, Major Barbara, Bewitched, The Winter's Tale* (RSC); in London's
West End: *Medea* (also on Broadway); *Trelawney of the Wells, Lloyd
George Knew My Father, The Dresser, Man and Superman*. Other recent
theatre includes: *The Black Rider* (also at San Francisco/Sydney), *Happiest
Days of Your Life, Separate Tables, Orpheus Descending, Lettice and
Lovage, Richard III, Candide, Tartuffe, The Fire Raisers, The Rules of the
Game*. Television includes: *Jewel in the Crown, The Singing Detective, As
Time Goes By, Tipping the Velvet, Uncle Silas, One Foot in the Grave, Dr
Who*. Film includes: *The Omen, Les Misérables, The Cook, the Thief, His
Wife and Her Lover, She'll Be Wearing Pink Pyjamas*.

Sam Holcroft
(Writer, *Dancing Bears*)
Recent work includes: *While You Lie* (Traverse) and *Pink* (as part of
the 'Women, Power and Politics' season, Tricycle). Other theatre work
includes: *Vanya*, Sam's radical adaptation of *Uncle Vanya* (Gate,
2009); *Cockroach* (co-produced by the Traverse and the National Theatre
of Scotland, nominated for Best New Play by the Critics' Awards for Theatre
in Scotland, 2008, shortlisted for the John Whiting Award, 2009); *Ned and
Sharon* (HighTide Festival, 2007) and short play *Vogue* (Royal Court,
2006). She received the Tom Erhardt Award in 2009, and was the Pearson
Writer in Residence at the Traverse, 2009–10. Sam is currently under
commission to the Traverse and Paines Plough.

Teya Lanzon
(Assistant Stage Manager, *Doris Day* and *Fatal Light*)
Teya is in her final year on the Stage Management BA (Hons) course at
Rose Bruford College. She previously trained at the BRIT School, gaining a
BTEC National Diploma in Technical Theatre. Her stage management work
includes: *The Vaudevillians* (Les Enfants Terribles, Croydon
Clocktower/Latitude Festival/Edinburgh Festival/New Players); *La Musica,
The Island* (Unicorn); *Oh! What a Lovely War* (Royal Academy of Music);
and various Stage Management roles within Rose Bruford College. She
was Entertainments Officer for the 2010 Rose Bruford Summer Ball and
worked on the production team for the 'Hope Festival' in Kent.

Emma Laxton
(Sound Designer)
Recent theatre design work includes: *Men Should Weep* (NT); *My Romantic
History* (Sheffield Theatres/Bush); *Travels With My Aunt* (Theatre Royal
Northampton); *Miss Lilly Gets Boned* (Finborough); *Sisters* (Crucible
Theatre Studio); *Off the Endz!* (Royal Court); *Like A Fishbone, The Whisky
Taster, If There Is I Haven't Found It Yet, 2nd May 1997, Apologia, The
Contingency Plan, Wrecks, Broken Space Season, 2000 Feet Away,
Tinderbox* (Bush); *Timing* (King's Head); *Ghosts* (Arcola); *Treasure Island*
(Theatre Royal Haymarket); *A Christmas Carol* (Chichester Festival
Theatre); *Welcome to Ramallah* (iceandfire); *Pornography* (Birmingham
Rep/Traverse); *Shoot/Get Treasure/Repeat* (NT).

Rebecca Lenkiewicz

(Writer, *That Almost Unnameable Lust*)

Theatre work includes: *Stars Over Kabul*, *The Lioness*, *The Typist*, *Her Naked Skin*, *Soho – A Tale of Table Dancers*, *The Night Season*, *Shoreditch Madonna*, *Blue Moon Over Poplar*, *Faeries*, *Justitia*. Adaptations include: *An Enemy of the People*, *Ghosts*, Stravinsky's *The Soldier's Tale*. Radio dramas include: *Sarah and Ken*, *Fighting for Words*, *The Man in the Suit*, *Caravan of Desire*. Her prose has been published in *Granta* and *The New Statesman*.

Susannah Lombardelli

(Design Assistant, *Charged*)

Susannah is a graduate of the Central School of Speech and Drama. She has a keen interest in devised writing and working with music within performance. She is the Associate Designer of the White Bear Theatre. Previous theatre work includes: *Lesbian Bathhouse* (Assembly Rooms); *She from the Sea* (Clean Break); *Lautes Licht* (Shunt Vaults); *Apartment 2012*, *Le Silence* (White Bear); *Emperor of the Moon*, *The House of Bernada Alba* (Embassy). Television and film work includes: *Jamie Oliver's Family Christmas* (Fresh One); *The Lease* (Prana Films); *Transit* (Pogo Films).

Isabella Mason

(AINE, *Fatal Light*)

Isabella is nine years old and lives in East Acton with her mum, sister and brother. She has been attending full-time stage school since the age of seven. Previous work includes appearances in *The Bill*, *Gok's Fashion Fix* and *Forgotten Children* for Channel 4. Isabella modelled for the launch of Stella McCartney's Gap Kids clothing line. She is thrilled to make her West End debut.

Ashley McGuire

(MAGGIE, *Fatal Light*)

Ashley appears as a Death Eater in *Harry Potter and the Deathly Hallows, Parts I and II*. Television includes: *Miranda*, *The Bill*, *Casualty*, *Law & Order UK*, *Murphy's Law*, *England Expects*, *EastEnders*. Other recent feature films include: *Baseline*, *Harry Brown*. Ashley is also one half of the comedy writers and performers Mackenzie & McGuire. Their critically acclaimed comic play *I'll Always Think of You That Way* (Pleasance Islington/ Pleasance Edinburgh, 2009) is in development as a sitcom with the BBC.

Lucy Morrison

(Director, *Doris Day* and *Fatal Light*)

Lucy is Clean Break's Head of Artistic Programme. For Clean Break, she developed and directed *it felt empty when the heart went at first but it is alright now* (Arcola); *This Wide Night* (Soho and tour, 2008; reprisal 2009). *it felt empty…* won the John Whiting Award 2010 and *This Wide Night* won the Susan Smith Blackburn Prize 2009. She was formerly Literary Manager of Paines Plough, where she worked with Dennis Kelly, Abi Morgan, Sarah Kane, Chloë Moss, Mark Ravenhill and Jack Thorne. Her other directing work includes: *Product* by Mark Ravenhill (Paines Plough at the Traverse/Royal Court Theatre Upstairs/European tour/Bush).

Chloë Moss

(Writer, *Fatal Light*)
Chloë's first play, *A Day in Dull Armour* (Royal Court), won the Royal Court's Young Writers Festival in 2002. Her next play *How Love is Spelt* (Bush) was awarded a special commendation by the Susan Smith Blackburn Prize. Chloë's other plays include *Christmas is Miles Away* (Manchester Royal Exchange/Bush) and *The Way Home* (Liverpool Everyman) In 2008 Chloë's play *This Wide Night*, produced by Clean Break and presented at Soho Theatre, was awarded the Susan Smith Blackburn Prize. The play was revived in Autumn 2009 at the Soho. Chloë is under commission to Clean Break, the Royal Court and the Liverpool Everyman. Chloë also writes for television and radio. She is currently working on projects for BBC3 and Touchpaper Television.

Dayna Moyes

(Assistant Stage Manager, *Taken* and *That Almost Unnameable Lust*)
Dayna is currently finishing her training in Stage Management BA (Hons) at Rose Bruford College. Whilst training, her work includes: *Up on the Roof* (New Wolsey); *Assassins* (Royal Academy of Music). With a passion for her job, she continues to work in regional and touring theatre.

Emma Noakes

(DAISY, *Doris Day* and POLICEWOMAN, *Fatal Light*)
Emma trained at the Oxford School of Drama. Theatre includes: *Wuthering Heights* (Birmingham Rep/UK tour); *Pygmalion* (Old Vic/Hong Kong Arts Festival); *The Sea* (Theatre Royal Haymarket). Television includes: *The Bill*, *Holby City*. Film includes: *The Other Boleyn Girl*. Emma's work in radio won the BBC Carleton Hobbs Award in 2006. Radio includes: *The Brothers Karamazov*, *Let Me*, *Maurice*, *For the Time Being* (Radio 3); *This is My Car Park*, *Inside the Whale*, *The Fall and Rise of Danny Clark* (Radio 4). Emma is also a reader for the RNIB Talking Books Service.

Rebecca Oldfield

(NOLA, *Taken* and WRITER, *That Almost Unnameable Lust*)
Rebecca trained at the Webber Douglas Academy of Dramatic Art. Theatre includes: *Pop*, *DEBBIE (Who couldn't catch a cold if she tried)* (Theatre503); *Freesia* (BAC); *Labour Pains* (Bush); *When Cheryl Was Brassic, Is Everyone OK?* (nabokov). Television includes: *The Silence*, *Doctor Who*, *Afterlife*, *Silent Witness*, *Holby City*.

Samantha Pearl

(RETARD / CHARITY, *Dancing Bears* and TUNDE, *Dream Pill*)
Samantha graduated from the Oxford School of Drama in 2009. Theatre includes: *Twelfth Night* (National Theatre Discover tour); *How to Be an Other Woman* (Gate). Television includes: *Snuggle Time*, *What Shall We Do Today* (Playhouse Disney). Film includes: *N25* (short).

Winsome Pinnock

(Writer, *Taken*)
Taken is Winsome's second play for Clean Break. Her first, *Mules*, was produced at the Royal Court and went on to be shown at the Ahmanson Theatre in Los Angeles and the Magic Theatre in San Francisco, as well as being presented in Australia and Jamaica. Her other plays include *A Hero's Welcome*, *Leave Taking*, *Talking in Tongues*, *Water* and *One Under*. She has also written for radio and television. Awards include the George Devine Award, the Pearson Award and the Unity Theatre Trust Award.

Rebecca Prichard

(Writer, *Dream Pill*)

Rebecca's plays include: *Essex Girls* (Royal Court); *Fair Game* (commissioned by the Royal Court and performed by the Royal Court at the Duke of York's); *Yard Gal*, co-produced by Clean Break and the Royal Court, and winner of the Critics' Circle Award for Most Promising Playwright in 1998; *Delir'ium* (Tricycle/Royal Court/Chichester Festival Theatre); *Futures* (Zurich Schauspielhaus/Theatre503). Rebecca's radio work includes: *Something Blue* (Radio 4); *A Good Doctor* (Women's Hour). She wrote *Dream Pill* whilst undertaking her AHRC Creative Fellowship at Lancaster University.

Rebecca Scroggs

(ANNA, *Doris Day* and JAY, *Fatal Light*)

Rebecca trained at RADA. She has appeared in *Detaining Justice* (part of the 'Not Black and White' season, Tricycle); *Danton's Death* (NT). Her work on screen includes *Hominid* for the BBC and the short film *15 Seconds*.

Caroline Steinbeis

(Director, *Taken* and *That Almost Unnameable Lust*)

Caroline is a freelance director. She won the JMK Award in 2009, and was on the Directors' Course at the National Theatre Studio in 2008, where she was also on attachment. Recent directing work includes: *The Cost of Things* (Public Theatre, NY); *Sports et Divertissements* (La Carrière du Normandoux, Poitiers); *Mad Forest*, *Photo Story* (BAC); *Mile End* (Southwark Playhouse/UK tour). Recent associate directing work includes: *Earthquakes in London* (NT).

Ros Terry

(Assistant Producer, *Charged*)

Ros has worked in stage management for ten years for a variety of theatre companies, touring both in the UK and internationally. She was Resident Stage Manager at the Bush Theatre for three years, where she loved working on new writing. She worked in Hong Kong for three months as Company Stage Manager on *The Nightingale* for the International Festival. Ros is currently Company Manager at the Young Vic Theatre. In 2009 Ros was accepted onto the Step Change Professional Development Programme, run by the National Theatre. She is currently on secondment with Clean Break.

Johanna Town

(Lighting Designer)

Johanna was shortlisted for the 2010 Whatsonstage Best Lighting Designer Award for *Speaking in Tongues* (Duke of York's). Recent theatre design work includes: *Romeo and Juliet*, *The Importance of Being Ernest* (Edinburgh Lyceum); *That Face* (Sheffield Crucible Studio); *Pride and Prejudice* (Theatre Royal Bath tour); *For King and Country* (UK tour); *The Hounding of David Oluwale* (West Yorkshire Playhouse/UK tour/Hackney); *The Tragedy of Thomas Hobbes* (RSC); *Carmen*, *Kátya Kabanová*, *Cinderella*, *The Secret Marriage* (Scottish Opera); *Fat Pig* (Trafalgar Studios/Comedy); *Giustino* (Trinity College of Music).

Sarah Tryfan

(Stage Manager, *Dancing Bears* and *Dream Pill*)

Sarah graduated from RADA in 2001. Recent theatre work includes: *The Arsonists*, *The Ugly One*, *The Stone*, *Over There* (Royal Court); *Stephen and the Sexy Partridge* (Trafalgar Studios); *Mine* (Shared Experience);

A Life in Three Acts (Traverse/Soho); *Miss Lilly Gets Boned* (Finborough). Recent opera work includes: *Semele* (Royal Academy Opera); *L'elisir d'amore, Falstaff, Norma, Capriccio* (Grange Park Opera); *Tête à Tête: The Opera Festival* (Riverside Studios).

Ony Uhiara
(DEAN / RAZOR KAY, *Dancing Bears* and KERRY, *Fatal Light*)
Theatre includes: *How to Be an Other Woman* (Gate); *Eurydice, In The Red and Brown Water* (Young Vic); *Noughts & Crosses, Pericles* (Ian Charleson Award Nominee), *The Winter's Tale, Days of Significance* (RSC); *Silverland* (Brits-Off-Broadway, New York); *Motortown, Fallout* (Royal Court); *Walk Hard – Talk Loud* (Tricycle); *Medea* (West Yorkshire Playhouse). Television includes: *White Van Man, Criminal Justice 2, Holby City, Hunter, Doctors, Rosemary and Thyme, The Bill, Holby City, Proof, The Crouches, MIT, Waking the Dead, The Vice.* Film includes: *Sixty 6, Venus.*

Danielle Vitalis
(ANGRY / BABYMOTHER, *Dancing Bears* and BOLA, *Dream Pill*)
Danielle has been performing on stage from the age of eight. She lived in St Lucia for many years, before moving to East London. She studied Performing Arts at NewVIc Sixth Form. Danielle starred in the BAFTA Award-winning educational series *L8R*. She recently performed on stage in *White Something* (Arcola). She also stars in the upcoming feature film *Attack the Block.*

Tessa Walker
(Director, *Dancing Bears* and *Dream Pill*)
Directing work includes: *The Red Helicopter* (Almeida); *Women on the Verge of HRT* (Derby); *Harm's Way* (Lowry, Manchester); *Black Crows* (Arcola, Clean Break); *Orange* (Script Cymru); *Matches for Monkeys* (Chelsea); *Debris* (BAC Critics' Choice Season, Theatre503/Traverse, Edinburgh/Staatstheater Biennale, Germany); *Blackout* (Soho); *The Watched* (tour); *The Supposed Person* (Le Petit Hebertot, Paris); *Hysteric Studs* (BAC/Theater Lab, Houston).

Clean Break

Clean Break is a theatre, education and new-writing company. We use theatre for personal and political change, working with women whose lives have been affected by the criminal justice system. Our ambition is for our theatre productions and education programmes to excite and invigorate audiences and to transform the lives of the women with whom we work. The Company was founded in 1979 by two women prisoners at HMP Askham Grange. It has grown over the past thirty-one years to become a critically acclaimed new-writing theatre company, highly respected for its education and training work. Clean Break is the only theatre company in the UK specifically working with women with experience of the criminal justice system and women at risk of offending due to mental health needs and drug/alcohol use. In 2010 the Company was nominated for a South Bank Show Award.

Our artistic programme
Clean Break produces an annual production, based on an original new-writing commission by an established playwright, on the theme of women and crime. The production tours to theatres and prisons, engaging audiences in the issues of women in the criminal justice system and enhancing Clean Break's role as a social commentator on the subject of women, crime and justice. Awards for recent productions include: Susan Smith Blackburn Award 2009 for *This Wide Night* (Chloë Moss) and the John Whiting Award 2010 for *it felt empty when the heart went at first but it is alright now* (Lucy Kirkwood).

Our education programme
Clean Break has been running its Education and Training Programme for over fifteen years, working with women from 18 to 60 years old. The programme is delivered at our purpose-built studios in Kentish Town. It comprises creative courses, financial assistance and specialist support, leading to qualifications, increased confidence and self-esteem, theatre and technical skills and pathways to further/higher education or employment. The programme aims to create a platform for learning and engagement for women who have not been in education for a significant amount of time, or whose experience of formal education was very negative.

Working in prisons
Clean Break has developed an expertise in delivering outreach and education work in women's prisons. Alongside the production tour, Clean Break delivers residencies and workshops within each of the prisons we visit. The residencies are extremely popular and we know from feedback that they are successful in engaging women, building confidence and self-respect and unlocking potential. We also deliver other theatre, new-writing and arts education projects in women's prisons. Two recent prison residencies have resulted in two Koestler Awards for stage plays.

Working with young women

The 'Miss Spent' programme has drawn on Clean Break's expertise to develop a gender-specific arts programme meeting the needs of young women, aged 14 to 21 years, involved in or at risk of offending. The programme has already been delivered successfully in London, Luton, Bradford and HMP Downview.

Make a donation and make a difference to more women's lives

Clean Break aims to bring about change directly in the lives of the women we work with and at a national level, by changing attitudes to women and crime through theatre, education and new writing. Our services are much in demand and we have ambitious plans for:

- more education work, affecting the lives of individual women and supporting them through their education at Clean Break and on to further or higher education, employment or voluntary work
- new-writing projects for professional and non-professional women writers
- increased work with young women offenders and those at risk of offending
- increased touring to theatres and prisons with accompanying education work
- supported writing programmes for women in prison
- training for artists and criminal justice professionals wanting to learn more about our ways of working

We invite you to contact us to discuss supporting one or more of these areas with a one-off or regular donation. We rely heavily on the generous support of our funders and donors. By making a financial contribution to Clean Break, you can make a difference to the lives of the women and their families. If you would like to discuss Clean Break's programme further and how you could get involved contact Lucy Perman MBE, Executive Director, on 020 7482 8600.

Alternatively you can donate directly online via our website at www.cleanbreak.org.uk

Clean Break
2 Patshull Road
London
NW5 2LB

Tel: 020 7482 8600
Fax: 020 7482 8611
general@cleanbreak.org.uk
www.cleanbreak.org.uk
facebook.com/cleanbreak
twitter.com/CleanBrk

Registered company number 2690758 | Registered charity number 1017560

Funded by Camden Council

Supported by
ARTS COUNCIL
ENGLAND

Clean Break would like to acknowledge the generous support of all its funders and supporters.
Clean Break is a member of ITC

For *Charged*

Production Team
Executive Director **Lucy Perman MBE**
Administrative Producer **Helen Pringle**
Head of Artistic Programme **Lucy Morrison**
General Manager **Louisa Norman**
Assistant Producer **Ros Terry**
Company Administrator **Molly McPhee**
Administrative Assistant (Artistic) **Amanda Castro**
Design Assistant for *Charged* **Susannah Lombardelli**
Assistant Stage Manager for *Charged* **Renee Ge**
Fight Director **Alison de Burgh**
Dialect Coach **Mary Howland**

Casting
Casting Consultant **Nadine Rennie CDG**

Marketing and Press Team
Marketing Consultants **The Cogency**
Press Consultant **Nancy Poole PR**

Set Construction and Painters
Factory Settings Ltd

Clean Break would like to especially acknowledge **Rose Bruford College** for their support and partnership in developing Assistant Stage Manager placements for Chloe R Brown, Teya Lanzon and Dayna Moyes. Clean Break also thanks the following for their support with *Charged*: Bendy Ashfield, ETT, RADA, Honeyrose Herbal Cigarettes, Kate Wood, Central School of Speech and Drama, ETC Lighting. Particular thanks go to Clare Lizzimore.

E V Crowe would like to thank Verity Hambrook for her support in the development of *Doris Day*.

Sam Holcroft would like to thank the following for their support in the development of *Dancing Bears*: Peaches Cadogan, Liz Carr, ROTA.

Rebecca Lenkiewicz would like to thank the following for their support in the development of *That Almost Unnameable Lust*: Perry Northage from Women in Prison, staff and prisoners at HMP Peterborough.

Chloë Moss would like to thank the following for their support in the development of *Fatal Light*: Jane Webb, Nicholas Rheinberg, David Hinchliffe, Deborah Coles and Maninder Jalaf from INQUEST, Ruth Bundey, Fiona Borrell, Susan J Royce, John and Denise Gunn.

Winsome Pinnock would like to thank the following for their support in the development of *Taken*: Michelle Richardson, Ellie Whitfield, Cecilia Hazlerigg of Hope House.

Rebecca Prichard would like to thank the following for their support in the development of *Dream Pill*: Jessica Southgate, Detective Inspector Steve Wilkinson, Detective Andy Desmond, Sally Montier, Professor Elaine Aston, Professor Helen Nicholson, the Arts and Humanities Research Council.

For Clean Break

Executive Director **Lucy Perman MBE**
Administrative Producer **Helen Pringle**
Head of Artistic Programme **Lucy Morrison**
Head of Education **Anna Herrmann**
Assistant Head of Education (Student Services)
   Jacqueline Stewart
Student Support Worker **Tracey Anderson**
Office Administrator **Mandy Base**
Student Support Worker **Ella Bullingham**
Administrative Assistant (Artistic) **Amanda Castro**
Finance Administrator **Won Fyfe**
Administrative Assistant (Education) (maternity leave)
   Verity La Roche
Theatre Education Manager **Rebecca Manley**
Theatre Education Manager **Laura McCluskey**
Company Administrator **Molly McPhee**
Locum Administrative Assistant (Education) **Val Nobbs**
General Manager **Louisa Norman**
Development Manager **Elly Shepherd**
Miss Spent Project Manager **Jo Whitehouse**
Outreach Worker **Ellie Whitfield**

CHARGED

DREAM PILL
Rebecca Prichard

FATAL LIGHT
Chloë Moss

TAKEN
Winsome Pinnock

DANCING BEARS
Sam Holcroft

THAT ALMOST UNNAMEABLE LUST
Rebecca Lenkiewicz

DORIS DAY
E V Crowe

DREAM PILL

Rebecca Prichard

Characters

TUNDE
BOLA

Setting

A basement.

TUNDE *is silently weeping into an old cushion shared between two mats.* BOLA *is concerned and looks between* TUNDE *and the audience, caught between a feeling of exposure and the possibility of help.*

BOLA   I don't know why she's crying

She just has days like this (*Shrugs.*) she's just having a bad day

(*To the audience.*) Why are you here?

BOLA *moves her mat a little farther from* TUNDE.

Tunde, I'm putting my mat over here

Tunde, I'm going to put my mat here but you can still touch it

You want me to comb your hair?

Why are you crying?

There's a room she doesn't like. Someone called her a bad name de.

BOLA *sees an empty chair in the audience.*

Are we allowed to sit here?
Tunde.
Tunde.
We can sit with them.

TUNDE *doesn't move, and* BOLA *is unsure.* BOLA *comes forward but then retreats a little to wait for* TUNDE.

Yeah. Those mats are hard
(*To* TUNDE.) Do you want to come and sit?

TUNDE *is curious but does not move, she remains watching* BOLA *however.*

You didn't do nothing to them. Sometimes the
men that come are angry but you didn't do
nothing to them

Want me to paint your eyes?

(*To the audience*.) You can ask her a question
She might come over here

BOLA *approaches the audience*, TUNDE *follows
a little distance behind.*

I'm nine she's ten
Do you know what her whole name is? It's
Yetunde. If you call her Tunde she says she
doesn't mind but really she does

TUNDE *shrugs.*

She's quiet. I'm loud

TUNDE   (*Quietly*.) I'm loud too

BOLA   I look after her sometimes

They look at one another, smile a bit.

But it depends. Sometimes she looks after me.

TUNDE   Yeah

BOLA *sees someone in the audience who has long
hair.*

BOLA   (*To a woman in the audience*.) You got long hair.
(*To* TUNDE.) She got long hair
(*To the woman*.) Can I touch your hair?

She reaches out almost to touch it then withdraws.

Why do you have long hair? Does it hurt? I know
someone that had long hair but she cut it off
because people were always pulling it. Has
anyone ever pulled your hair?

She got long hair

TUNDE *is amazed* BOLA *almost touched
someone in the audience and has not been told off.*

*She approaches. She holds a necklace in her hand
that's broken. She shows it to the audience.*

(*As if the audience member broke it.*)You broke it.
You'll pay!
Not really!

They laugh a little and TUNDE *places the broken
necklace in a hiding place.*

(*To audience member.*) I have a big belly

She mimes a protruding belly.

It's got no hairs though

BOLA *and* TUNDE *approach the audience again.*

Are you spirits?

TUNDE	We're not spirits
BOLA	We're real She's ten. I'm nine
TUNDE	No, I'm nine too
BOLA	When will you be ten?

TUNDE *shrugs.*

TUNDE	Soon.
BOLA	What will you get?
TUNDE	Sparkly clothes
BOLA	I'm going to get clothes.

BOLA *nods as if to say 'Good?'*

TUNDE	Yeah, it's good
BOLA	Yeah.

BOLA *crouches down to inspect the audience's
shoes.* TUNDE *copies her but is not quite as bold.*

(*To the audience.*) I like your shoes. They're nice.
        I like what you're wearing. It's nice.

TUNDE   Are you going to work here?

BOLA   …if you are going to work you should probably change your clothes

TUNDE   Yeah.

BOLA   Get set

TUNDE   Baff up bit

BOLA   You will like working here

TUNDE   We like it, is alright

BOLA   Iss easy. Is better than washin' feets

TUNDE   Is better than that.

BOLA   You can relax here

TUNDE   You can unwind

    All day long

BOLA   Unless it's night-time

TUNDE   You can see films and

BOLA   You can see yourself in a film, like dream

TUNDE   Or play games

BOLA   And if you are sad you can hear music

    BOLA *turns on a small transistor radio, a favourite song of theirs is playing, and they call out the name of the singer:*

BOTH   Beyoncé!

    BOLA *is about to raise the volume on the radio. A reverberating sound as Dawud throws a box down the stairs offstage. Both* TUNDE *and* BOLA *freeze and startle but then pretend not to.* TUNDE *turns the music down.* TUNDE *and* BOLA *go and peer up the stairs.*

BOLA   You'll bring him down

TUNDE	No he's going back up
BOLA	He will come down again

Pause. BOLA *eyes* TUNDE *slightly authoritatively.*

You got to drink more water

TUNDE *sips from a litre bottle of water in the corner.*

She forgets

Another sound of Dawud shifting and moving things around.

(*To audience.*) Das okay

TUNDE	Das jus Dedeh
BOLA	He is bossman
TUNDE	He nice but
BOLA	He shouts all the time.
TUNDE	He shout so he forgot how to speak

They wait for the audience's reaction.

BOLA	He brings us gifts. You will like him
TUNDE	Yeah sometimes he will bring you gifts
BOLA	Sometimes we sleep with Dedeh …sometimes he just sleeps with me
TUNDE	And me as well
BOLA	But he never touches us He just takes his watch off
TUNDE	Yeah, and in the mornings he coughs
BOLA	He lets us watch de screen
TUNDE	He can let you sit with men
BOLA	He will let you sit with men

TUNDE   (*Miming someone weighted down.*) Some are
          heavy

BOLA   They get eyes that are open but never look at
          nobody

TUNDE   People are sad because their clothes are too heavy
          for them. When they take them off they go
          'phpphoo'. Their skin is cold and white with
          blue bits

BOLA   Their eyes are like this

          *Demonstrates shifty eyes gliding over surround-
          ings without landing on anything.*

TUNDE   Yeah, they got eyes like this

          *She demonstrates small distant eyes with her
          fingers.*

          *They begin to imitate how the English accent is
          different from their own accents.*

BOLA   They say 'down'

TUNDE   'Round'

BOLA   'Brown'

TUNDE   'Sit down'

BOLA   'Come round'

TUNDE   'Your skin is brown'

BOLA   Their blood is white and sticky

          I can tell you how to make them go quick. Just go
               'yeah-yeah-yeah' like that
          Or you can make a pose

TUNDE   (*Something that indicates anal.*) Boom boom

BOLA   (*Something that indicates frontal.*) Bang bang

TUNDE   (*Something that indicates oral.*) Yum yum

          *They make various poses during the above and
          laugh at one another.*

BOLA	You don't have to touch them you can jus' dance for them
TUNDE	Yeah you can dance like this

They switch on the radio again. They dance around, pulling moves.

BOLA	Bang bang
TUNDE	Boom boom
BOLA	Yum yum
TUNDE	We move for you
BOLA	We get Bakassi
TUNDE	We get move

More sounds offstage of loading and unloading gear. BOLA *and* TUNDE *turn the music down to listen, reminded of their 'work'.*

BOLA   You must change

BOLA *pulls out a glittery dress for* TUNDE.

Dedeh brought dis for you…

TUNDE	Or you can wear't?
BOLA	He will get mad.

TUNDE *shrugs.*

He says you are lazy. (*To the audience.*) He says she is lazy.

TUNDE   (*Shrugs.*) I am lazy.

Pause. TUNDE *approaches the audience.*

Sometimes Dedeh threatens to beat us

BOLA	But it doesn't hurt when he beats us
TUNDE	Yeah we just say it doesn't really hurt
BOLA	Because he's a bit gay

TUNDE   Yeah he's gay

          *They glance at each other and wonder if the
          audience will let them get away with saying this,
          they laugh a bit.*

BOLA   He says that one day he'll set fire to this room
          But he won't

TUNDE   Will he?

BOLA   He can't set fire to room because all our stuff's
          here

          BOLA *runs to their 'hiding place' in the room and
          draws out a necklace and amulet.*

TUNDE   Important sturvs
          Dis tings we found here

BOLA   Dis a necklace dat protect you against demon

TUNDE   Is necklace we get for protection

BOLA   Dis one – (*The necklace.*) my antie gave me

TUNDE   She gave ha with a wish

BOLA   Das blessing
          She say
          Ki Olorun Ki Ofu Li

BOTH   Emmi Gigun ['*May God bless you with a long
          life*']

TUNDE   Do you know what it means?

BOLA   Is blessing

TUNDE   Antie.

BOLA   Dis a shoe we found

          TUNDE *also wants the audience's attention so
          shows something she has found.*

TUNDE   Dis a link for button... (*She holds the cufflink to
          her ear as an earring.*)

BOLA	She don't know my antie but she misses her as well. Because I told her about my antie. You miss her too isn't it?
TUNDE	Yeah
BOLA	But she don't know ha She have no antie, is not ha real antie
TUNDE	But she like antie She smell of paffin
BOLA	Paraffin for lamp

They breathe in, enjoying imagining the smell.

TUNDE	And cooking
BOLA	She get smooth back from all de children she carry. Dey smooth a special place for me to sit, vey comfortable. When she sleep she talk for ha, but is my antie
TUNDE	Do you know that it is dangerous to talk in your sleep?
'	Cos if you talk in your sleep, spirits can enter de
BOLA	Dedeh talks in his sleep – is dangerous
TUNDE	He doesn't know it's dangerous
BOLA	Yeah. Sometimes he talks in his sleep, he goes like this
	Mmmngh
TUNDE	Nnngh Mama
BOLA	I'm not bad Mama

They laugh a bit.

TUNDE	It's because he has problem – e nor kolo [*crazy*]
BOLA	It's because he's sad inside.
TUNDE	Dis a shoe we found here. After we was sleeping
BOLA	It wasn't de before

TUNDE   Is a shoe we found

          They hold and inspect the man's shoe, and offer it to the audience to inspect.

BOLA   And dis a cigarette... butt... a cigarette butt

TUNDE   Dey was not de when we was sleeping. It is ghosts... dey enta

BOLA   Is because – she talks in ha sleep so demon – dey enta here

TUNDE   They make smoke

          BOLA *points to an air vent.*

BOLA   They come through there

          TUNDE *points to the stairs.*

TUNDE   Dey leave de. Dey are from de sound in dis pipe. They make sound from de throat

BOLA   Dey come through here – (*Indicates vent again.*) They travel de – (*Indicates pipe.*) they leave de – (*Indicates exit.*)

TUNDE   Das why we get protection. Das why we use dis

          TUNDE *holds the amulet.*

          Ha antie get one too. She hold it for protection

BOLA   Is blessed – De priest bless it. She gave us dis Have you ever been to winch? She like madam. You go pay dem for protection before you go on journey, is like blessing. Dey protect you from demon and hex.
          My antie take me to protect me on long journey, she pay dem

TUNDE   First you mus be in a darken room

BOLA   No no no wait – first you must – de madam, she must see you for daylight – she look at you, look you up and down.

TUNDE   Oh yeah

BOLA   Your antie take you

BOLA *positions* TUNDE.

Tan de, tan de [*stand there*]

BOLA *pretends to be the madame.* TUNDE
pretends to be BOLA. BOLA *leans back, arms
folded, and regards* TUNDE *as if she were a bad
smell, and occasionally pokes and prods her.*

Hmmmmmmmmm – (*She clicks her tongue or some
other mannerism, skeptically.*) No bad. No
bad. Tun [*turn*]. Tun. Comot for hia. Mm.
Show me you teeth. Mm

TUNDE *smiles wanly to show her teeth.*

TUNDE   Ha breath tink. De woman get dead animal fe
mout'

BOLA   (*As Madame.*) Na bad. She strong. Nothing do her,
she not bad at all.

TUNDE   Ha teeth – 'e be like say God put dem for mouth
wid bat – dey confuse.

BOLA   (*As Madame.*) Tun. Dis ha nylon na be silk, her
diesel na be four-star unleaded, but she dey
kampke, na endurance go test ha when she go
UK's.
If she stay here 'e no go betta for her – she juss
dey here laik dele [*being idle*], myself I got
green cad, visa, papas, passport, immigration
– na wahala [*trouble*] – Lady, I have bin dey
myself – shine your eye – (*She shows off or
rattles jewellery.*) Pepper don rested and
crested wid me [*I've made a lot of money*],
seen, I get pound I get dollar, I get euro, I get
lira, do you know Folake's child, dat speak
five langwish, she speak am all, she get euro
like turn water fe tap

> Mek you kuku tink on it. I get so much money, smell me – (*She sniffs her armpit or hand.*) I stink of it. We arrange all fe you – no wahala, no long ting [*no problem*], you nor lift hair – but I – you must – abeg mek you add extra – I say make you add extra, na so so wahala for carry pickin, de trouble wey my eye see nor be small. I mus' settle priest, police, custom, soljah, dem nor chop [*consume or eat*] dollar small-small

TUNDE   De madame – she sell heap and powder

BOLA   Dagbo visa [*fake visa*]

TUNDE   Barks and herbs

BOLA   SIM card

TUNDE   Medicine for constipation

BOLA   Battery and freshna

TUNDE   Paper for Yankee and Jand

BOLA   If you fit fe journey den de madam go take you to priest

TUNDE   Dis how priest protect you from demon

BOLA   She tek you – dem put you
          in darken room

TUNDE   You mus' wash
          You have fe drink whisky

          TUNDE *pretends to take a clipping of* BOLA*'s hair.*

          Dem take clipping of your hair

BOLA   Dey draw circle round you

          She mimes drawing a circle.

          Dey take your cloth

TUNDE   No no no – you must undress. Dey take your panties

BOLA	Dey put it for jar. Dey cut you here and here
TUNDE	Dey go put am for shrine
BOLA	No dey float jar for water, because your journey you go fly ova water
TUNDE	And you must swear –
BOLA	Swear
TUNDE	You pay back de contrac'
BOLA	Ev'ry dollar, cos if you ansa boss –
TUNDE	If you nor wuk hard
BOLA	If you nor earn Oga [*boss*] money
TUNDE	If you speak out
BOLA	If you run away
TUNDE	If you ansa
BOLA	Dey go chase you down

They go up close to the audience, warning them directly.

TUNDE	Demon can enta your mind
BOLA	Dey can enta your dream
TUNDE	Dey can punish you
BOLA	Dey can steal you thought and mek you mad
TUNDE	Dey can dry up you thot
BOLA	Kill you, wake you, kill you 'gain
TUNDE	Give you disease
BOLA	AIDS
TUNDE	Dey can kill you mama
BOLA	Leave her bodi wey by roadside
TUNDE	Dat she torn apart by dog

BOLA   Yeah – zombie can enta your dream. Tunde has
                seen zombie
            when she sleep with Dedeh
            She see inside ha own dream
            For film
            Tell dem
            She hear sound

TUNDE   No…
            De is – you can jus' see dey fingers, dey touch
                you. When you are sleeping. When you take
                pill. Dey get fingers dat are white like bones.
                De flesh rot way. Dey touch you hair wey you
                left am for priest. You can hear dey breath, is
                heavy. Cuz dey are dead.

BOLA   She say you can be wake, dey can wake you but
                you still sleeping. You cannot move. Only you
                eye.
            Tunde can make herself die and come back to life
                like spirit

            TUNDE *shakes her head as if to say not really,*
            but this is partly out of embarrassment.

            Like abiku

TUNDE   No is you
            No you do that

BOLA   She can put spells on people. (*To* TUNDE.) Isn't
                it?

            TUNDE *is unsure whether to accept this.*

            You know this sound – (*She puts her ear to a pipe*
                or imitates its sound.) That's where she goes
                (*To* TUNDE.)… you said
            (*To audience.*) And she goes where the dreams in
                the dream pills are born
            (*Beat.*) One time, one time
            she had a faint into a trance

TUNDE   Yeah – I fell to the ground –

BOLA   Show them
            Her eyes go went all inside – (*Demonstrates*.) You
                just saw the whites of her eyes.

            TUNDE *feels proud of her new status as a spirit,
            but also exposed.*

            Show them what you did with your eyes

            TUNDE *briefly imitates herself before a trance.*

            What do you see?

TUNDE   Nothing. Just faces

BOLA   But sometimes they hold onto her, and they talk to
                her
            What do they say?

TUNDE   They say this world is not real
            They say the people of this world don't really
                want us here
            And we going home

BOLA   Will you go back?

            BOLA *waits expectantly for a reply. Again*
            TUNDE *is unsure how far to enter this idea.*

            Sometimes she just falls into a trance, but she
                can't just choose, can you?

            TUNDE *simply stares back at* BOLA.

            She can't fall into trance whenever she wants
                because the spirits decide when to call her,
                and she has to be careful because they might
                not let her back so...

            As BOLA *speaks* TUNDE *allows her eyes to
            retreat, showing just the whites of her eyes, and
            she falls to the floor behind* BOLA. BOLA *is
            shocked and goes to inspect her. She looks at her
            flickering eyes and puts her hand near* TUNDE*'s
            nose to feel for any breath.*

            Tunde? Tunde?

Just as she is about to listen to TUNDE*'s heart*
TUNDE *jumps up with a roar and* BOLA *rolls
away and they collapse laughing.*

TUNDE   Ra!

BOLA   Ah!

They play-fight a little, then become serious again.

TUNDE   Dem touch you, pick you as you sleep, move you

BOLA   You nor know

TUNDE   Dey leave mark on you body

BOLA   You nor wan sleep. You ketch fear
        Dis why you get special pill

TUNDE   Dream pills

BOLA   Is a special pill for protection – Dedeh give it

TUNDE   Is a pill which catch demon inside
        It make you faint
        It go like this
        Demon move
        They look like dis

*She imitates something which could either be a
spiritual state or, equally, a sexual one.*

De eyes go like dis
(*She imitates an ecstatic fluttering of eyelids.*) for
        film

BOLA   Yeah – dey flutter and dey roll

TUNDE   Dedeh can capture dem inside screen

BOLA   And we get mark
        See?

TUNDE   Yeah – when you wake you have mark

They show the audience marks on their arms.

BOLA   Here and here

TUNDE   and here

They show the audience other marks they have found on their bodies – on their hands, backs or legs. These could be friction burns, bite marks, bruises or other strange marks.

Dis were not here before

BOLA   Dey are real, because if you go to their place, when you sleeping, they can mark you

TUNDE   Is it?

They wait for a response.

BOLA   They nor know
Dedeh says you wake up in a place, diff'rent place, wid diff'rent room and it is still real. Is dat true? Are we still real?

TUNDE   Are you?

BOLA *and* TUNDE *receive no reassurance from the audience. They transfer their fears onto the pipes and vents in the room.*

BOLA   Zombie enta de

TUNDE   Dey leave de

BOLA   Dey are in pipes

TUNDE   Dey hold meetings

BOLA   Dey talk

TUNDE   Dey chant

BOLA   It is in de throat
Dats why we wan leave dis room

TUNDE   Das why

BOLA   Dedeh says one day he will fly us home

TUNDE   We tell him we nor like dis room

BOLA   We tell him we wan fly home

TUNDE   He say he will fly us home

BOLA   Do you know when you take off in a plane pessin
        look smaller dan you hand

TUNDE   Dedeh says we go fly from here

BOLA   De first time she saw screen was when she fly. She
        thot it was a dream coming from de back of a
        person's head, because de TV was in the seat.
        Ca she a bush person

TUNDE   No you are

BOLA   Ca where she is from dey nor have TV nor
        machine fe washin'

TUNDE   No das you!
        You thot there was a spirit in de toilet. Because it
        makes a loud sound she thought it will bite ha
        and spit ha out of the plane

BOLA   The air hostess is spirit
        She is like a zombie

TUNDE   She has no shape

BOLA   She is shaped by ha clothes

TUNDE   She has to walk up and down smiling

BOLA   She smiles on all the food to take de taste away

TUNDE   She smiles to keep de bubbles in your drinks

BOLA   She smiles hard
        And she bring you all de Fanta you want

TUNDE   Have you ever been in a plane?

BOLA   We fly so high

TUNDE   When you are up that high you look out de
        window it is like you are looking down on a
        pan of boiling water

BOLA   You can watch film!
        And when you land it is like you are going to land
        on a golden snake

TUNDE	We like going in planes You can relax
BOLA	You can unwind
TUNDE	Dey bring you nuts
BOLA	Is free
TUNDE	People put dey chairs back like dis

TUNDE *mimes*, BOLA *copies*.

| BOLA | Yeah like dis |

BOLA *pretends to put an eyemask down and close her eyes*. TUNDE *may copy her, or pretend to wear a neck cushion*.

You must be careful not to kick de chair in front

You have to put a belt on

TUNDE	And dere is a sound which goes – (*Holds her nose*.) 'bong'
BOLA	Dedeh say he is going to take us in a plane again when we go home
TUNDE	We going to watch film from back of a pessin's head We going to fly Away from Uke's. She nor wan us
BOLA	UK is a place
TUNDE	Nor Uke is a person. With many child. We nor reach de yet
BOLA	Nor she is a place
TUNDE	London is a place. Uke is a person
BOLA	Nor...
TUNDE	Anyhow we go escape
BOLA	(*To audience*.) Have you ever seen *Prison Break*?

TUNDE	When Dedeh let us sleep wid him, he let us watch film
BOLA	He like *Prison Break*
TUNDE	Yeah we like *Prison Break*
BOLA	Dedeh like it
TUNDE	It's our favourite, he likes de guy wid tattoo
BOLA	We watch film

They speak with 'Americanised' Nigerian accents.

'You're not going to believe it Big Daddy'

TUNDE	'I already don't. What?'
BOLA	'I'm getting you out of here'
TUNDE	'You're what?'
BOLA	'You going deaf on me?'
TUNDE	'It's impossible'
BOLA	'Over here: the vault, open it'

BOLA *indicates the air vent.*

TUNDE	'I can't, sir, it's too heavy, it's jammed'
BOLA	'Well bust it open, goddammit. On second thoughts I'll do it myself'

BOLA *pretends to kick down a grate or the air vent.* BOLA *and* TUNDE *pretend this sets off an alarm and then pretend to be police entering with guns.*

TUNDE	GET DOWN! GET DOWN ON THE FLOOR! DON' MOVE!
BOLA	Police van SWAT team siren I SAID FREEZE! (*As prisoner, to* TUNDE.) Come, we go escape
TUNDE	PUT YOUR HANDS ABOVE YOUR HEAD DON' MOVE I SAID FREEZE

BOLA	We go escape UK now!
	BOLA *beckons to* TUNDE *to escape with her,* TUNDE *drops her mime and joins* BOLA.
	There is a tunnel somewhere
TUNDE	Dere is a grate
	They look up at the air vent.
BOLA	I climb for you
	BOLA *attempts to climb on* TUNDE*'s shoulders. She falls down and they start to use the space, clambering on or under tables, boxes, or on each other, as they describe their escape.*
TUNDE	We fly for vent
BOLA	I go stand on your shoulder We go through vent
TUNDE	Up de. We pull.
BOLA	We climb inside
TUNDE	We run tru tunnel
BOLA	Run tru many tunnel
TUNDE	Is all dust and demon
BOLA	We nor know which way to turn
TUNDE	We face fire
	They jump down from a stack of boxes and hide under another surface, perhaps then moving among the audience.
BOLA	We inside people legs
TUNDE	We carry go, Tru all de people leg Tru desert
BOLA	Tru bandit
TUNDE	Tru immigration We go fast

BOLA	We go far!
TUNDE	Ova water
BOLA	Under sea
TUNDE	Tru tunnel
BOLA	Over mountain
TUNDE	In air
BOLA	We scream
TUNDE	Aaa! Home! Away away
BOLA	Waaaah! Far!
TUNDE	Far! We run
BOLA	We see light
TUNDE	We keep run!
BOLA	De stars are waiting on de odder side!
TUNDE	Dey waited for us!
BOLA	We jump into them!
TUNDE	They is more than you can count
BOLA	And light

Brief celebratory screams, then they remember where they are and look at the door fearfully. An intercom buzzes offstage. Loud voices are heard indistinctly as they shout over the intercom. Street traffic can also be heard momentarily. A few moments later another intercom buzzes near the basement. BOLA *and* TUNDE *know they have been putting off necessary preparations. They look at the dress.*

You go change now

TUNDE *drags her feet.*

Hurry

BOLA *runs to peer up the stairs.*

He is coming. No lie.

TUNDE *believes her and a shaking panic overtakes her as* BOLA *helps her get dressed.* BOLA *sees* TUNDE*'s distress.*

I can go?
I can go instead of you?

TUNDE   (*Sad.*) He put the dress for me

BOLA   Here

BOLA *helps* TUNDE *with her make-up.*

Wait

BOLA *applies make-up to* TUNDE*'s eyes and helps* TUNDE *finish getting ready.* BOLA *watches as* TUNDE *leaves.* TUNDE *walks falteringly in shoes that do not fit her well.* BOLA *is left in the room.*

BOLA *returns to* TUNDE*'s mat. She feels self-conscious once the audience witness* TUNDE*'s exit. She plays with her fingers, twisting them, and looking around her. She continues to glance at the door with anxiety.*

I don't know what they are doing in there
Now I have to drink the water

BOLA *goes to a litre bottle of water.* BOLA *returns to* TUNDE*'s mat. She's quiet for a while.*

Sometimes you can know there is rain when
    people have it on their faces, and their clothes

Sometimes I think could there ever be a kind of
    rain to blind people. Blind de eyes

It is in the Bible. There is a story of creation.
    Yeah.
Do you know the story of creation?
I know a story of creation

The audience do not respond so she begins a
dialogue with herself.

(*To herself.*) Sit de, sit still.
Did you know that God made the earth?
When God made the earth
He did a spell
No
When people come
He made stars, he made dem into eyes
You have to sit next to people
And in the beginning all things could speak.
>   Including stones and plants. But everything
>   got too loud and so God stopped it
When they sit next to you, you can't sit far away
>   you have to sit close like this?
Like that.
They put their arm here.
'Sit in my lap.'
And they put something inside
'Can I sit in your lap?'
They have dark hair and pink bodies
So
Even the stars sang but they were so high up no
>   one could hear. Dey was windows dat God
>   look through.
People shouted all the time. There were so many
>   noises with all the plants singing they had to
>   shout. That there was singing. And they all
>   got coughs and were sick and vomited up a
>   whole load more people
And then I was born I peed and I made a river and
>   flowed all over the earth
And then they bathed. And that was the only thing
>   they had to bathe in
And the people got angry with the earth and cut
>   off all her skin, so now she's bare and naked
And then – and then you come in, and you say to
>   Dedeh, 'I didn't do anything bad'
'No I didn't do anything bad'

And then you say
'Would it make you sad?'
Ask me ask me if it would make me sad to stay
    here.
(*To audience member.*) Would it make you sad to
    stay here?
'Yes'
She did what I said
She says 'Don't you want to go home?'

BOLA *imagines a conversation with an audience
member, but remains in her own space and in her
own world of play, without approaching anyone,
the following dialogue is with herself.*

Okay, let's go home.
'Thank you.'
'Bye'
'Bye.'
'I'll see you whenever.'
'Yeah, all right.'
'Okay.'
And then pretend like I asked you if I could stay
    here.
'Stay here for ever?'
Yes this place.
And she says 'There are immigration people?'
    And I say 'Never mind'
And what do you say?
(*She looks at the audience.*) They are a dream pill
I am a dream pill (*Sadly.*) I will stay here for ever

TUNDE *enters. Her dress is ripped and her face
smudged and bruised.* TUNDE *stands in shock for
a while.* BOLA *looks at her. It has become darker
outside and the sounds upstairs seem distant.*

Dey nor wan you…?

Pause.

Dem touch you, dem send you down?
Did he bring you pill?

TUNDE *nods her head. She searches her dress for the place Dawud usually hides the dream pills.*

Did you save some for me?

TUNDE *bites half her pill and gives the remaining half to* BOLA.

They are real.

TUNDE *nods.*

Is good

TUNDE   Yeah

BOLA   (*To audience.*) Are we a dream pill?
Did we dream this room?

TUNDE   Will you dream me?

BOLA   Can you?

TUNDE   Can I be in your dream?
Are you real?

BOLA   Are we?

Blackout.

The End.

FATAL LIGHT

Chloë Moss

Characters

JAY
MAGGIE
AINE
POLICE OFFICER
KERRY

One

MAGGIE*'s house.* MAGGIE *and a young female* POLICE
OFFICER *sit at opposite sides of the table.*

MAGGIE. What happens now?

The POLICE OFFICER *pulls a card from her pocket and
hands it to* MAGGIE.

POLICE OFFICER. If you call this number, they'll be able to
help.

MAGGIE. You're shaking. (*Beat.*) What'll they do?

POLICE OFFICER. They can… answer your questions. Put
you in touch with the right people.

MAGGIE. 'The right people'?

POLICE OFFICER. The prison governer, legal representation.
(*Beat.*) The coroner.

MAGGIE. Do you have to do this much?

POLICE OFFICER. No, not – Sometimes. Only sometimes.

MAGGIE. It must be very difficult.

Pause.

POLICE OFFICER. Not as hard as – I can't even imagine –

MAGGIE. Shouldn't you have someone with you? Is it normal,
this, doing it on your own?

POLICE OFFICER. It… depends.

MAGGIE. What on?

Beat.

POLICE OFFICER. Numbers. We're a bit pushed today.

MAGGIE. I thought they had to send two. I thought it was the law. I don't know why, I suppose I'm getting that off the telly. (*Beat.*) It doesn't seem fair. How old are you?

Beat.

POLICE OFFICER. Twenty-one.

Silence.

The next steps are – You need to… before they can issue any – You'll have to formally identify Julie's body.

MAGGIE. Her name's Janine.

Pause.

POLICE OFFICER. I'm so sorry.

MAGGIE. They said she'd be safe.

Silence.

Was there – Did she… leave anything?

POLICE OFFICER.…

MAGGIE. A note?

Beat.

POLICE OFFICER. I… don't know.

MAGGIE. So there might have been?

POLICE OFFICER. There might have been but they didn't say.

Silence.

(*Gesturing to the card.*) If you call that –

MAGGIE. Do they all cry straight away? Or start screaming? D'you think I don't care?

POLICE OFFICER. No. I think you're… in shock.

MAGGIE. 'Shock'? No, I'm not in shock. I'm not shocked. (*Beat.*) She got four years.

Silence.

Did you meet her?

POLICE OFFICER. No. (*Beat.*) I'm from – They ring the local station. So we can get to you quickly.

MAGGIE. Right, because it's a long way, isn't it? For someone to get here from the prison. Takes me over four-and-a-half hours, door to door. I get two buses to Euston then it's a two-and-a-half hour train ride then a thirty-minute bus ride. It'd be quicker if I got the Tube to Euston but I haven't got the Tube in years. I'm claustrophobic. The last time I was on one, there was a power failure and it got stuck in the bloody tunnel for fifteen minutes, which I know isn't very long at all but if you suffer with it like I do then it's an eternity. An absolute living hell. This poor old woman had to calm me down, I was nearly hammering on the windows, I would have got out and crawled along the tracks in the dark if I could, I felt so desperate. (*Pause.*) I felt so completely desperate.

MAGGIE *lets out a howl. The* POLICE OFFICER *searches for something to say.*

POLICE OFFICER. Do you want me to get you something? A glass of water or something?

MAGGIE (*composing herself, calm again*). A glass of water? No. I don't want a glass of water.

Silence.

She's got a little girl. My granddaughter. She's here with me, it's just the two of us. I'm not sure... when you go now, I'm not sure what to do.

POLICE OFFICER. Is there anybody I can ring for you?

MAGGIE. No. No, thank you. (*Beat.*) Will you – Do you come back?

Pause.

POLICE OFFICER. No. If you call that number then –

MAGGIE. The number. Yeah. You've told me all this. It's just, my head...

The POLICE OFFICER *goes to leave.* MAGGIE *leans forward to hug her. She seems startled but lets* MAGGIE *put her arms around her, keeping her arms down by her sides. The* POLICE OFFICER *leaves.* MAGGIE *sits down at the table, broken.*

Two

MAGGIE *sits, slicing an apple and reading the paper.* AINE *runs in on her hobby horse, running circles around the table.*

MAGGIE. Pack it in. You're making me dizzy.

AINE *stops.*

You're getting too big for him now, aren't you?

AINE. It's a girl.

MAGGIE. For her then. That's for babies. You're not a baby, are you? (*Beat.*) Are you?

AINE *stares at* MAGGIE.

Course you're not. You're a big girl now. (*Beat.*) Have some apple.

MAGGIE *holds the apple out.* AINE *takes a piece and eats it.*

Don't swallow the pips.

AINE. Why not?

MAGGIE. Because a whopping great tree'll grow in your tummy and come out of the top of your head.

MAGGIE *laughs.* AINE *is silent. She puts the piece of apple back on the table.*

I'm only having a joke with you.

AINE. You shouldn't make jokes like that with children.

MAGGIE. I'm sorry. (*Slaps her own hand*.) Silly Nanny.

AINE *stares at her*.

AINE. How long have I got to stay here for?

Beat.

MAGGIE. I don't know yet. Until Mummy gets better.

AINE. Will she get better soon?

MAGGIE. Yeah, she will, course she will. But this is nice.
(*Beat*.) Isn't this nice? Me and you spending time together.

AINE. My friend's nanny lives with her. She's called Danielle.
Her nanny bought her a pink DS.

MAGGIE. A pink what?

AINE. DS. It's a games console.

MAGGIE. Lucky Danielle.

AINE *sits down and picks her book up to read*.

That looks good, is it good?

AINE *nods. She flicks through and shows* MAGGIE *a page*.

AINE. This is where I'm going to on holiday.

MAGGIE *laughs*.

MAGGIE. The Emerald City? You'll have a job getting there,
sweetheart.

Silence.

Do you want me to read it to you?

AINE *shakes her head*.

AINE. I can read it to myself.

MAGGIE. That's because you're very clever.

Beat.

AINE. Mum says you don't like coming to ours any more.
That's why we haven't seen you for ages.

Silence.

Why don't you like coming to our flat?

AINE *picks up a piece of apple.*

MAGGIE. I don't *not* like – I think… I think when you're older… you might be able to understand things a bit more. How people are sometimes. Families.

AINE. Are you my family?

MAGGIE. Yes. Of course I am.

Silence. AINE *spits the apple pips into her hand.*

AINE. I'm going to plant these.

MAGGIE. That's a nice idea.

MAGGIE *watches as* AINE *leaves.*

Three

JAY *lies in her prison cell. She is wearing a vest top. Her arms are bandaged. Opposite,* KERRY *is fast asleep, the covers pulled right over her head. The prison door creaks open and* AINE *appears. She pads over to* JAY *and shakes her shoulder.* JAY *sits up.*

JAY. What you doing?

AINE. I couldn't sleep.

JAY. You shouldn't be here. They don't let children in.

AINE. Nobody saw me, I walked straight past. They didn't even look.

JAY. You'll have to go.

AINE. Can't I get in with you? Just for a bit.

Beat. JAY *pulls the covers back and* AINE *climbs in, snuggling down with her.* JAY *holds on tight.*

(*Gesturing to* KERRY.) What's she like?

JAY. She's alright, y'know.

AINE. What did she do?

JAY. Stole stuff. (*Beat.*) She's got a little boy.

Beat.

AINE. My feet are freezing.

JAY. Rub them on my legs.

AINE *rubs her feet on* JAY*'s legs.*

(*Loudly.*) Ow. (*Whispering.*) When was the last time you clipped your toenails?

AINE *giggles.* JAY *shushes her.*

You'll get me in big trouble, you will.

AINE. I had to come, I miss you too much.

Beat.

JAY. How's Nanny?

AINE. She's alright but she can't cook.

JAY. I know, she's useless, isn't she? (*Beat.*) But she's good at other stuff. She goes on about shit but she loves you.

AINE. Do you still love me?

Beat.

JAY. I love you so desperately I feel like my heart might stop sometimes.

AINE. I know.

JAY. Do you?

AINE. Yeah. Course I do.

JAY. You'll be a good girl for her, won't you?

AINE. Yeah.

> JAY *holds* AINE. *Slowly,* AINE *pulls herself away and leaves.*

> JAY *is alone. She gets out of bed, sits up, paces the floor, lies down on the floor, gets up and flies at the door banging and screaming.*

Four

KERRY *stirs, she sits up, throwing the blanket off herself.*

KERRY (*shouting*). Oi. Pack it in.

> JAY *stops. She turns to* KERRY, *almost relieved.*

Fuckin' headcase.

> JAY *stands, staring at* KERRY.

They won't come. I'd save your energy, mate. Gonna need it.

> KERRY *picks up a magazine and starts to flick through it.*

JAY. I'm not violent.

> *Silence.* KERRY *cracks her chewing gum loudly.*

I haven't done anything violent.

KERRY (*still flicking through the pages of her magazine*). Couldn't give a shit what you've done to be honest, mate. (*Beat.*) Long as it's nowt to do with kids. Could. Not. Give. A. Monkeys.

JAY. Is it okay if I talk to you?

> *Silence.*

Please can I talk to you?

> *Pause.* KERRY *puts the magazine down, swings her legs around and sits on the edge of the bed, staring at* JAY.

KERRY. Go on then. Talk.

JAY fishes in her pocket and pulls out a photograph of
AINE. She hands it to KERRY.

JAY. S'my little girl.

KERRY hands the photo straight back and lies down again.

KERRY. Sorry. No. Can't do that. Can't get into all that shit.

JAY. I just want to tell you about her.

KERRY. You're not the only one with kids, love.

Beat.

JAY. It's my first night. I think I might do something. I need to
talk to someone.

Beat.

KERRY. You can probably see Sharon. At some point.

JAY. Who's Sharon?

KERRY. Woman for your head.

JAY. Where is she? Can I see her now?

KERRY snorts with laughter.

What?

KERRY. It's half one in the morning. They do nine-thirty to
five-thirty, Monday to Friday, them lot. So if you wanna top
yourself or have a fucking breakdown, keep it office hours,
yeah?

JAY pulls the blanket over herself. KERRY watches as the
blanket moves. She stands and marches over to JAY, pulling
the blanket away. JAY is digging a pen into her arm.
KERRY grabs the pen off her.

And if you wanna rip holes in your arm, go and do it in the
bog.

KERRY puts the pen in her pocket.

S'fuckin' gross.

JAY *huddles in a ball on the bed, she pulls the blanket back over herself, she begins to wail.*

It's for your own good. They catch you doin' that shit, they'll stick you in solitary and that's the last fucking place you wanna be. (*Beat.*) If your head's not right before you've been in there, it's definitely not gonna be right after. Send a fuckin' Buddhist monk loopy, solitary.

JAY *is calmer, she sits up.*

Pull your sleeves down.

JAY *does so.*

JAY. Please can I talk to you? I'm frightened. I've got a little girl.

Beat.

KERRY. What's her name?

Five

An interview room in a police station. JAY *sits at a table opposite an invisible detective. A tape recorder plays.*

JAY. Janine Emma Hill. (*Beat.*) You can call me Jay, though, I don't mind.

Pause.

Twenty-fifth of April, nineteen eighty-six.

Pause.

The Aylesbury Estate.

Pause. JAY *sighs.*

Flat 33b, Thurlow Street on the Aylesbury Estate, Walworth SE17 2UZ, London, England. Great Britain. The World.

Pause.

No, I don't. I'm not laughing.

Pause.

Just me and my daughter. Aine. She's six.

Pause.

She was at school. I'm not gonna start a fire when she's in the fucking house, am I? I wasn't trying to hurt anyone.

Pause.

I poured lighter fuel on the floorboards and threw a lit match on them.

Pause.

It wasn't the *whole* flat, it was a section of the floor but it just went up, I wasn't expecting it to be like that. I got scared so I phoned the fire brigade. There's an old woman downstairs.

Pause.

No. I wasn't drunk. A can. Two cans, tops. (*Beat.*) I'm not a fucking alky. It just helps sometimes, that's all. Softens things.

Pause.

Sometimes.

Pause.

I've never laid a hand on her. I wouldn't. I'd never touch a hair on her head. I'd die for her. I would. She's just this... (*Long pause.*) You know when you go Burger King? Or McDonald's. KFC? Shit like that? (*Beat.*) D'you empty your tray into the bin or d'you just leave it on the table?

Silence.

She empties it by herself. She's seven and when she's finished she picks it up and she takes it over and she puts it in the bin. I don't tell her. I don't even do it myself. I used to work in Burger King and it fucked me off when people cleaned up after themselves. I like to keep busy, y'see. It is *fucking* soul-destroying, that job, specially when you're not on the tills. You just have to walk around with a brush and one of them little flippy-bin things with the handle and clear up shit. Which is okay, long as there's shit to clear up. People think they're being helpful but they're not.

Anyway, she doesn't know that. All she's thinking is that it's important to clean up after yourself. It is important not to rely on other people to mop up your shit.

You have to learn to look after yourself. (*Beat.*) It doesn't sound much, I know, but it makes my head ache, I'm telling you. We're walking down the road one day together. Couple of years ago. I swear down, she's like… four. And she looks up at me, face all scrunched up and she goes. Hang on… She goes… 'In my imagination, sometimes I feel sorry for somebody but I don't know who they are. I haven't got a sad face but I just feel a bit… urgh. Do you ever get that?' (*Beat.*) Four years of age. I swear. Her soul is like this – Her heart, man. Her little big heart. She cripples me. She just totally does me in.

Silence.

Can I go home now please?

Six

JAY *is on her hands and knees, scrubbing at an invisible stain on the floor.* AINE *is helping, rubbing the floor with a cloth, half-heartedly.*

AINE. I can't even see anything.

JAY. It's filthy.

AINE. There's nothing there.

JAY *stops, exasperated.*

JAY. Do you remember when the man came round?

AINE *nods.*

Do you remember what he said?

AINE *shakes her head.*

He said we have to keep it clean in here. Didn't he? He said we've got to look after each other. I've got to look after you. So, what d'you think I'm doing?

Silence.

What d'you think I'm doing?

Silence.

What d'you think's gonna happen if I don't keep it clean? (*Pause, louder.*) Aine. What do you think is going to happen?

AINE. I don't know.

JAY. They'll take you away. Alright? (*Beat.*) D'you want them to take you away?

AINE *shakes her head, pulls her knees tighter to her chest.*

Well, shut up then. Let me get on with it.

JAY *continues to scrub,* AINE *goes and fetches her book, holding it up in front of her face but keeping one eye on* JAY.

JAY *notices. Feeling guilty, she stops scrubbing for a moment.* AINE *seizes the opportunity and stands up, the book outstretched.*

AINE. Can you show me where we're going on holiday again?

Beat. JAY *puts down the brush, pulls* AINE *onto her knee and flicks through to a particular page.* AINE *puts her arms around* JAY *as she points.*

JAY. There. That's where we're going.

AINE. How will we get there?

JAY. On a plane. How else we gonna get there?

AINE. When?

JAY. One day. When Mummy's saved up, I promise. Just me and you.

AINE. Danielle says there's no such place.

JAY. Well, Danielle would say that. She's jealous, isn't she? Coz she can't go there. You should just tell Danielle when she starts saying things. Tell her you don't wanna know. Tell her to get out of your head.

AINE. She says loads of things.

JAY nudges AINE off her knee then continues scrubbing.

JAY. I know, but you just wanna ignore her. Seriously.

AINE. She says stuff about heaven.

JAY. What about heaven?

AINE. She says that in heaven, when you get there, everyone looks the same so you can't ever find who you're looking for.

JAY. This is what I mean. She talks rubbish. Always got her nose pressed up against that bloody Game Boy.

AINE. It's a DS.

JAY. Whatever. They're bad for you, those things. They stunt your growth – (*Taps head.*) In here.

AINE. She never lets me have a go on it.

JAY. Good. She's doin' you a favour. You should tell her to shove it where the sun don't shine and stop talking nonsense about heaven.

Pause.

AINE. What if I'm looking for you and I can't find you?

JAY stops for a moment.

JAY. Do you think that's gonna happen? Do you honestly think I'd let that happen?

AINE shakes her head.

That is never gonna happen.

JAY carries on scrubbing.

I'm gonna have a word with her mother. Soon as you're back at school, I'm gonna speak to her. Tell her. She wants to get her to bed earlier. Hardly any surprise she's got all this gloom and doom in her head. Sleep deprivation, innit? Sends you round the twist.

JAY *stops scrubbing for a second to push her hair from her face*. AINE *reaches down quickly and snatches the brush away*.

What are you doin'?

AINE. You said we could play hide-and-seek.

JAY. Later.

AINE. You said it ages ago.

JAY. Give me that back. Now.

AINE (*re: the floor*). It's clean.

JAY. No it isn't. Give me it back.

AINE *holds the brush behind her back*.

What have I just said to you? What did I just say about the man?

Silence.

I'm warning you.

AINE *stands firm*. JAY *is furious*.

Right, fine. Is that what you want then?

AINE. Please stop it.

JAY (*shouting*). Is that what you want? You want to get taken away? I can take you now. Get it over with. I'll take you myself instead of them coming around and kicking that door down in the middle of the night. Coz that's what'll happen. Do you want them to come and get you in the middle of the night?

AINE *stands stock-still, terrified*.

Get dressed. (*Beat*.) Go on, get your *fucking* coat on.

Silence.

(*Screams.*) Move.

JAY *goes to grab* AINE. AINE *throws the brush at* JAY'*s feet.* JAY *stops. Picks it up and starts to scrub again.* AINE *curls up in a ball, distressed.*

You're such a selfish little girl sometimes. (*Beat.*) I'm doing this because I love you. I'm doing it to keep us together.

AINE *doesn't respond, she's curled tight.*

Don't you want us to be together?

Still no response. JAY *stops scrubbing and moves along the floor, wrapping her arms around* AINE.

(*Softer.*) Don't you want us to be together?

AINE *nods slowly.*

You gotta be a good girl, then, haven't you? Listen to what I tell you. Put your arms around me.

AINE *hugs* JAY *stiffly, reluctantly.* JAY *holds her face.*

Do you want a mega-quick go of hide-and-seek? Five minutes, tops. Then I've got to carry on with this. Okay?

Silence.

Aine, d'you wanna go or not? (*Beat.*) Why are you being like this?

AINE *nods, more to appease* JAY *than wanting to play.* JAY *stands, puts her hands over her eyes. Counting down from ten.* AINE *stands confused, just watching* JAY *for the first few counts.*

Five, four, three –

Reluctant, AINE *goes off to hide.*

– two, one. Coming, ready or not.

JAY *takes her hands away from her eyes.* MAGGIE *is standing in front of her.*

Seven

MAGGIE*'s flat*. JAY *is shaken, anxious*.

JAY. Where is she?

MAGGIE. She's having a nap.

> JAY *tries to storm past* MAGGIE. MAGGIE *stands in her way*.

JAY. What d'you think you're doing?

MAGGIE. She'll be awake soon, leave her.

> JAY *stops, suppressing fury*. MAGGIE *is tense, wary*.

I can stick the kettle on for us. Have you had lunch?

JAY. I'm not hungry.

MAGGIE. What's up? What's going on?

JAY. Someone's been round. Some prick from Social Services. Some fucking *man*, telling me how to be a mother. Giving me *instructions*.

MAGGIE. Saying what?

JAY. Saying the flat's a mess.

MAGGIE. What else?

JAY. Does it fucking matter what else? I've got some stranger in my home, uninvited, telling me I'm a dirty bitch –

MAGGIE. He called you what?

JAY. Said I need to keep things 'nice and clean'.

MAGGIE. Well, there's a bit of a difference.

JAY. Is there?

MAGGIE. Course.

> *Beat.*

JAY. You don't seem all that surprised.

MAGGIE. What's that supposed to mean?

JAY. Please don't insult me, please be honest. For once in your life.

MAGGIE. You've lost me. Honestly, you've completely –

JAY (*shouting over* MAGGIE'*s shoulder*). Aine.

MAGGIE. Leave her. Just… let's sort this out first. Please.

JAY. There's nothing to sort out, I just want to take my daughter home. Get her away from you.

MAGGIE. What are you talking about? She loves it here. She's been happy… we've had a lovely morning.

JAY. I bet you have.

MAGGIE. Course we have.

JAY. I know what you're trying to do. (*Beat.*) What have you been telling him?

MAGGIE. Who?

JAY. That fat prick from before. Coming round, waving his clipboard in my face. Having the cheek to smile at me.

MAGGIE. Nothing. I haven't said a thing, I wouldn't dream of – Why the hell would I do something like that?

JAY. It's not gonna fuckin' happen. I'm her mother. If you carry on like this, you're not gonna see her at all. It's your decision, but I'd tread very fucking carefully if I were you.

MAGGIE. Stop it. Stop it now.

MAGGIE *takes hold of* JAY.

This is nonsense. You know it is. It's nonsense.

Weary and upset, JAY *doesn't resist as* MAGGIE *puts her arms around her.*

It's gonna be okay. Nothing's gonna happen, I promise.

JAY *stays in* MAGGIE'*s arms, comforted for a few moments before steeling herself and pulling away.*

JAY. No, no no no. I know what you're doing.

MAGGIE. I'm not doing anything.

JAY. You're *never* going to get her. *I'm* her mother. You're never gonna fucking have her. You are never *ever* going to have her.

Beat.

MAGGIE. I swear to you. I swear on my *life* –

JAY. Promising you weren't going to interfere. Soon as she comes along you're all over me like a rash, like you give a shit. You're so fucking transparent.

MAGGIE. Like I give a shit? About you? How can you say that?

JAY. Oh fuck off. If it wasn't for her, you wouldn't care if you never saw me again.

But you've got to put up with me. Because if you don't put up with me then you know that you can't get to her, but d'you know what's hilarious?

MAGGIE. I don't 'put up' with you.

JAY. D'you know what's hilarious?

MAGGIE. This is so… uncalled for. I feel shocked. Have you been taking your tablets?

JAY. Oh shut up. You're fucking uncalled for, d'you know what's hilarious? I'm asking you a question.

MAGGIE. Have you been taking them?

JAY. Do. You. Know. What. Is. Hilarious?

Silence.

She doesn't even like you.

MAGGIE.…

JAY. She told me. Can't fucking stand you. Doesn't trust you. Thinks you're all about yourself.

MAGGIE. No. (*Beat.*) Please don't do this. Not again. Please, not when everything's been so –

JAY. I know the way your head works. You're a fucking schemer. I know what you're like, what you're really like. But you've fucked it for yourself now. You've completely fucked it.

MAGGIE starts to cry, helpless.

MAGGIE. I'm not like anything. I promise you I'm not like anything. Whatever it is, whatever's in your head, it isn't true. It isn't real.

JAY. There's nothing in my fucking head. Apart from you and I know you're real, I can fucking see you, you cunt.

AINE appears, awoken by the row. MAGGIE and JAY shut up immediately.

Hello, sweetheart.

JAY holds her arms out, AINE hugs her.

Did you have a nice sleep?

AINE. Why are you shouting?

JAY. Who's shouting? We're not shouting, are we?

Beat.

MAGGIE. No.

JAY. See? Okay, babe, get your things together.

AINE. Can't we stay here for a bit more?

AINE looks to MAGGIE, who is unsure how to react.

JAY. No. Aine, come on. (*Beat.*) Say goodbye to Nanny.

AINE stands and gives MAGGIE a hug. MAGGIE holds her tightly. JAY holds a hand out and AINE takes it.

Let's go home.

MAGGIE and JAY hold one another's gaze.

Eight

*JAY's flat. JAY is seven months pregnant. She stands opposite
MAGGIE, who can't take her eyes off JAY's bump.*

MAGGIE. You must be six months.

JAY. Seven.

> *Silence. MAGGIE continues to stare.*

> Say something.

MAGGIE. I don't know what to say. I can't think straight.
(*Beat.*) Seven months?

JAY. I know. I'm sorry.

> *Silence.*

> I thought you might try and talk me out of it.

MAGGIE. It's a bit bloody late for that.

JAY. Exactly.

MAGGIE. And that's insulting. Actually. (*Beat.*) Why would you
think that? Why would you think that I'd try to 'talk' you out
of it? Like I've ever been able to talk you out of anything.

JAY. Don't be like that. Don't be angry.

MAGGIE. No. I'm not – I'm… I don't know what I am.

JAY. Just be happy.

MAGGIE. I'm worried. Actually. That's what I am. Worried
sick. This is a… huge responsibility.

JAY. You're kidding? Is it? I never even knew. Cheers for that.

> *JAY smiles.*

MAGGIE. This is not funny. How can you possibly find this
funny?

JAY. I'm not laughing.

MAGGIE. You're smirking.

JAY. I'm *smiling*. Breaking the ice.

MAGGIE. You're breaking my bloody heart. I thought you were dead.

JAY. Don't be dramatic, I phone you.

MAGGIE. Once a month. If that.

JAY (*shrugs*). Let you know I'm not dead.

MAGGIE. There you go, you can be so…

JAY. Well, I'm not, am I? I'm more alive than I've ever been. Feel that.

MAGGIE *stands. She puts her hand tentatively on* JAY's *stomach.*

She's like a little jumping bean.

MAGGIE. It's a girl?

JAY *nods.* MAGGIE *sits back down.*

JAY. I've picked a name and everything.

MAGGIE. What is it?

JAY. Aine ['*Aww-n-ya*'].

MAGGIE (*mispronounces*). Aww-ner.

JAY. Ya, ya… Aine.

MAGGIE (*corrects*). Aine. (*Beat.*) Aine. I'll have to write it down. I'm gonna look stupid, aren't I? People ask me what my own granddaughter's name is and I can't even remember how to say it. What am I gonna look like?

JAY. You'll look even more stupid getting a fucking bit of paper out. (*Beat.*) What people anyway?

MAGGIE. People people. I don't know. Anyone. Neighbours. (*Beat.*) Celia.

JAY (*tuts*). You care too much what fucking Celia thinks.

MAGGIE. Oi.

Silence.

JAY. What d'you reckon, then? (*Beat.*) Her name. D'you like it?

Beat.

MAGGIE. I dunno. Sounds a bit like something you rub on a bite. (*Beat.*) Where'd you pluck that from?

JAY. I didn't 'pluck' it. I chose it. Carefully. (*Beat.*) It means 'radiance'. Aine is a goddess of light.

MAGGIE. Oh, Christ on a bike.

JAY. She encourages human love and takes the form of a red mare that nobody can outrun.

MAGGIE. I wish you wouldn't read those books.

JAY. What books?

MAGGIE. Those ones from that shop that sells those things, those 'dreamcatcher' things. And those bloody awful Josh sticks.

JAY. Joss sticks.

MAGGIE. They bloody stink. Get right to the back of your throat.

Silence.

What about the father?

JAY. Less said about that…

MAGGIE. Oh, for Christ's sake, Jay.

JAY. You can talk.

MAGGIE. Exactly. You should know better.

JAY. I didn't realise I was that big a mistake.

MAGGIE. That's not what I meant. You know that's not what I meant, don't go twisting my words. (*Pause.*) What happens now, then? With your medication?

Beat.

JAY. I take a lower dose. Make sure I keep going the doctor's.

MAGGIE. And you do go? You keep your appointments?

JAY. Course I do.

MAGGIE looks as though she might cry, holds it back. She looks around at JAY's flat.

MAGGIE. Least it's not… too bad here, is it?

JAY. I painted it myself.

MAGGIE. Did you? You did a good job.

JAY. Ta.

MAGGIE. Could be a bit warmer.

Long silence. MAGGIE pulls an envelope from her bag and hands it to JAY.

JAY. What is it?

MAGGIE. A card.

MAGGIE half-shrugs, gestures to JAY's bump. JAY opens the card, a twenty-pound note falls out. She picks it up.

JAY. Thanks. (*She reads from the card.*) 'Let your soul shine… like the sunshine.' (*Pause.*) Did you make that up?

MAGGIE. No. I got those 'women's' tea bags you told me about. They're meant to make you feel 'consciously alive', whatever that means. I thought you'd like them. They're those ones that you just sort of leave in the cup. Y'know, it's not like normal tea where it stews and gets that film on the top. You can just leave it in there. And you don't need milk. Or sugar. You just add water then you leave –

JAY. *Herbal* tea is basically what you're talking about. They're basically just *herbal* tea bags.

MAGGIE. Yeah, I suppose they are. Women's ones. I got myself some. They're quite calming apparently. Caffeine-free. (*Beat.*) They've got string on them and on the end there's this

little bit of paper. Each one's got a sort of message on it. And
the one I was having this morning, said that. 'Let your soul
shine like the sunshine.' (*Beat*.) I thought it was nice and I
wasn't sure what to put, so... I wrote that. (*Beat*.) They're a
hell of a lot more expensive but that's because they're
organic. I didn't know you could even get organic tea.
Anyway, I've brought you some. And some other stuff. Food.
Normal, not organic or anything. Biscuits, few little bits.

*MAGGIE picks up a carrier bag and holds it out. JAY
hesitates before taking it from her.*

I hope it's alright. I wasn't sure what to bring. You'll have to
write a list for me. Things you need. For next time. (*Beat*.) If
you want.

JAY. Yeah. That'd be nice. Thanks.

Silence.

MAGGIE. I've missed you. (*Beat*.) It's been torture, actually.
It's not a lecture. I'm not having a go. I'm just telling you. I
miss you. So badly.

Beat.

JAY. I miss you.

MAGGIE. Really?

JAY nods.

I'm sorry.

JAY. What for?

MAGGIE. If I've ever – The things I've done wrong.

JAY. You haven't done anything wrong.

MAGGIE. I've let you down.

JAY. You haven't let me down.

MAGGIE. I don't know, sometimes, what the best thing to do
is. And it cripples me. (*Beat*.) You'll know all about that
soon. When Aine comes along.

Beat.

JAY. It's gonna be alright, y'know?

MAGGIE. Is it?

JAY. Yeah. I feel better. I think everything's gonna be alright.

MAGGIE. You look good. You look well. (*Beat*.) You look beautiful.

JAY. I feel it.

Silence.

MAGGIE. Now things are – With the baby. I dunno, maybe I can help. Be around. If you want me to be. Not to interfere. Just to… be there.

JAY. That'd be good, yeah.

MAGGIE. Just to be there.

JAY. Yeah, I'd like that.

Silence.

MAGGIE. 'Aine.' (*Beat*.) It's nice, actually.

The End.

TAKEN

Winsome Pinnock

Characters

DELLA, *forties*
NOLA, *twenties*
NANA NOLA, *seventies*

Setting

The play takes place in the living room of a council flat in the present day.

*We are in the living room of a council flat in North London. A
sofa that has seen better days – a general air of neglect in the
room. On the floor there are two boxes full of junk. A sequinned
dress is draped over the sofa and on the floor beneath are a pair
of dance shoes. There is a pram beside the sofa.* NOLA *is
alone. She peers inside the pram and gently rocks it before
returning her attention to the room.* DELLA *enters wearing an
apron and rubber gloves. She holds a duster and can of
furniture polish. She stands in the doorway watching* NOLA,
who is poking through one of the boxes. NOLA *picks up a pair
of china shepherdesses and puts one in her pocket, and puts the
other back in the box. She stands and looks around the room as
though searching for something. She appears to find it as she
picks up a silver framed photograph. She gently brushes the
surface of the picture with her fingertips as though removing
dust from it.* DELLA *moves away from the door.*

DELLA (*calling offstage*). We've got another five hours yet,
Mum. Don't you worry. I'll let you know when it's time.

NOLA *quickly stuffs the picture inside her jacket as* DELLA
enters.

Do you watch *Strictly Come Dancing*? It's a big deal in this
house. Mum never misses it.

DELLA *gets on with her dusting as she speaks. Throughout
the scene she is constantly moving – dusting or adjusting
something. She can't sit still.*

She can't remember a lot of things, but she never forgets that
Saturday night is dance night.

NOLA. I've never seen it.

DELLA. You should. All them lovely dresses. All them fit
bodies. It adds a little bit of glamour to our lives, doesn't it?
You get hold of your friend yet?

NOLA. I can't find my mobile.

DELLA. You're all right to stay here and wait for a bit. As long as you don't mind me getting on with this.

NOLA. I'm just grateful to have somewhere to sit.

DELLA. I couldn't have you standing out there with the baby. Not after you had to climb all them stairs.

NOLA. I can't believe that girl. She's got a mind like a sieve. I rang her two days ago to remind her we was coming.

DELLA. Good thing that bloke give you a hand, weren't it?

NOLA. Good thing you let us in.

DELLA. It's not your day, is it? And now you can't find your mobile.

NOLA. I had it when I come out the station, cos I called Julie.

DELLA. But she didn't answer?

NOLA. I thought she was most probably in the bath or something.

DELLA. When I was your age that was the worst thing: to let your best mate down.

NOLA. She's always doing it. Girl's a nutcase.

DELLA. Yeah?

NOLA *suddenly stops and stares straight ahead, her eyes wide, her voice like that of a robot.*

NOLA. Do not be alarmed. I come in peace. I have temporarily taken over the body of your friend to bring you a message from the planet Zoran.

DELLA. You all right?

NOLA. A message especially for you, Della Campbell, because you have been chosen by the elders.

DELLA. Chosen? Me?

NOLA *relaxes*.

NOLA. That's how she goes on. I was scared out of my skin the first time she did it to me.

DELLA. You had me going there. I couldn't put up with a
     friend like that.

NOLA. I feel sorry for her. She had a rough childhood.

DELLA. That isn't your fault, is it? How d'you know my
     name's Campbell?

NOLA. I can read your mind. Think of a number.

DELLA. Three.

NOLA. You're not supposed to tell me.

DELLA. Saved you the embarrassment. (*Laughs*.) Read my
     mind. (*Kicks the box which has her name on it*.) Read the
     label on this, more like.

NOLA (*searching her bag again*). It's got to be in here
     somewhere.

DELLA. It's always the way, isn't it? I spent a good half hour
     looking for my glasses the other day. You never guess where
     I found them?

NOLA. Where?

     DELLA *taps her nose*.

     (*Laughs*). No!

DELLA. Not that I make a habit of wearing glasses. They don't
     suit everyone, do they?

NOLA (*continues to search her bag*). You moving house?

DELLA. I want to get rid of all this junk. Mum's lived here for
     ever – she never throws anything out. I've got a bloke coming
     tomorrow to take this lot. He had two boxes last week. See
     these? (*She picks up a china shepherdess*.) Looks like butter
     wouldn't melt in her mouth, don't she? Like all she's got on
     her mind is skipping down the hill chasing fluffy little lambs,
     but I reckon her and her sisters are at it like rabbits as soon as
     my back's turned because every morning I come in here and
     there's hundreds more of 'em all over the room.

NOLA. Your mum don't mind you throwing them out?

DELLA. I told her when I moved in: it's either them or me.

NOLA. And she chose you?

DELLA. She didn't have much of a choice: someone has to take care of her.

NOLA. Must be weird moving back in to a place you grew up in.

DELLA. You're telling me. Talk about memories. Sometimes I feel like a teenager again.

NOLA. How long you been here then?

DELLA. Six months? I'll have to get that wallpaper off next. Give the place a lick of paint.

NOLA. Where did you live before?

DELLA. Oh, here and there. I move around a lot, me.

NOLA. I'm like that. I've got itchy feet.

DELLA. Yeah?

NOLA. I can't stay put in one place for too long. I love travelling. I plan to go round the world once I've saved enough money.

DELLA. That's not so easy when you've got a kid.

NOLA. She'll come with me. I'll strap her on my back before taking her up a mountain.

DELLA. You'd be best off waiting till she's grown up before you go doing anything like that. Kids need security.

NOLA. You got children?

DELLA. Nah.

NOLA. Why not?

DELLA. It just never happened.

NOLA. But you wanted it to?

DELLA. Maybe I did. Maybe I didn't.

NOLA. Does that mean you did?

DELLA. That means it's none of your beeswax.

NOLA. I'm being nosy, en I? (*Slight pause.*) Oh no. My purse is gone too.

DELLA. I hope whatever you've got isn't catching. I've had enough bad luck, me.

NOLA. I had a hundred quid in there.

DELLA. A hundred quid, yeah?

NOLA. Me and Julie were gonna go down the shopping centre to buy stuff for the baby's party.

DELLA. That's no good, is it? You don't think it was that bloke, do you?

NOLA (*realising that it must have been*). Shit. Why am I so fucking…

DELLA. There's a lot of criminals round here. It could've happened to anybody.

NOLA. But it never, did it? (*She starts to cry.*)

DELLA. Come on. It's only money.

NOLA. It's her birthday in two weeks. I wanted to make it special.

DELLA. What about I lend you the money?

NOLA. But you don't even know me.

DELLA. I know enough to trust you'll give it back, won't you?

NOLA. I can't take money from you.

DELLA. No? Oh, I'll bet you can. (*Sudden change of tone.*) Greedy little bitch, ent yer?

NOLA *cries out as* DELLA *grabs hold of her.*

I don't mind if you steal a few bits and bobs off me cos I was gonna throw them out anyway, but you got to go that little bit further by trying to con me out of a few quid an' all.

NOLA. Let go of me. I haven't taken nothing.

DELLA. You must think I'm like all those old women you've pulled this scam on. I had you sussed the minute I see you on my doorstep.

Shakes NOLA.

NOLA. Ow! That hurt!

DELLA. You met your match here today, young lady. Think you're the first person to think up something like this?

She feels for the ornament in NOLA*'s pocket and takes it out. Then she pulls the photo out of* NOLA*'s jacket.*

I was working this scam before your mum and dad even got off together down the local disco. Do you really think you'll get anything for this load of crap?

She pushes NOLA *out of the way.* NOLA *rubs at her shoulder.*

Still, I don't suppose it matters when you're chasing a fix, does it?

NOLA. Are you calling me a junkie?

DELLA. I can tell just by looking at you – right little crack-head.

NOLA. You don't know nothing about me.

DELLA. I met hundreds of girls just like you in Holloway, in Askham Grange.

NOLA. You been inside?

DELLA. I might look like a Stepford wife, but I only come out of rehab nine months ago. That weren't no walk in the park, I tell yer. All I had when I come out was the clothes on my back. That's given you something to think about, ennit? Don't you go thinking you're different, it won't happen to you, because it will. Get out now while you're young and got your whole life ahead of you. Bet some bloke put you up to this. I'm right, en I? Bet he turned you on to the drugs an' all. Him and the crack whispering sweet nothings in your ear, promising you the world. Well, let me tell you something: they're both lying cunts who just want to control you. And if you don't get out quick one or both of them will destroy you.

NOLA. Have you finished with the Public Information Broadcast?

DELLA. I just hope some of it's got through your thick little skull. Now get out of my flat and don't let me see you round here again cos if I do I'm gonna be straight on to the police.

NOLA *goes over to the pram.*

And make sure you take care of that little baby of yours. (*Relenting.*) Look, hold on.

DELLA *lifts her apron and takes money from her trouser pocket and hands it to* NOLA.

NOLA. What's that for?

DELLA. Get something for the kid. Go on, take it.

NOLA *takes the money.*

NOLA. Can I have that picture?

DELLA. You're a strange one, ent yer? What do you want with a picture of a total stranger?

NOLA. I like it.

NOLA *takes the photograph.*

(*Looking at the photograph.*) You look really nice. Happy. I love that dress. All the colours of the rainbow. You're at a holiday park, ent yer? One day it rains and you're soaked through. The material sticks to your skin. You look like a mermaid. When the wind blows the dress puffs out like a parachute and you tell us to hold you down so that you don't take off. I've never seen you so happy.

DELLA (*realisation dawning*). No way.

NOLA. You tell me I'm sweet as the cherry on top of my birthday cake. You throw me up in the air five times and I feel that sick lurching feeling when I fly up and I shout at you to stop because I think I'm going to fall and hit the floor, but by the third lift I'm giggling and I can't stop.

Pause.

DELLA. Shut up. You can't be.

Pause. NOLA *can't look at her.*

You tried to con me.

NOLA. I didn't... I wanted you to... You owe me.

DELLA *is at a loss.*

DELLA. I can't believe this.

NOLA. You never even recognised me.

DELLA. It's been a long time. (*Slight pause.*) You got a new family now, ent you?

NOLA. So what? You don't want me here?

DELLA. Of course I do. I been longing to see you for twenty years. I didn't hurt you, did I? Let me have a look at that.

NOLA. No, don't, I'm all right.

Pause.

DELLA. What you doing here? I thought you'd forgotten all about me.

NOLA. Like you forgot about me?

DELLA. You went to a nice family, didn't you? You were better off.

NOLA. I had my own bedroom. Three square meals a day, two holidays a year, but the best holiday I ever had was at that holiday park with you.

DELLA. Don't say that. It makes me think your life's been shit when you say that.

NOLA. I come here for her – (*Referring to the pram.*) I want her to know that her mum didn't come gift-wrapped one Christmas. I want her to know I come from someone else's flesh and blood.

DELLA. You've got good parents.

NOLA. But they're not you.

Pause. DELLA *is secretly chuffed.*

DELLA. I wouldn't have thought you'd remember that holiday. I can hardly remember it meself. You must have a photographic memory.

NOLA. I remember it because it was brilliant. You were brilliant. You made us laugh the whole time. I just remember giggling non-stop.

DELLA. Didn't take much to make you laugh. All I had to do was tickle you. Didn't even have to touch you – just the thought of it would make you laugh. I only had to do this.

She tentatively and lightly touches NOLA*'s shoulder. Nothing happens. Pause.*

You still in touch with little Trevor?

NOLA. I was for a few years, but then he disappeared.

DELLA. What do you mean he disappeared?

NOLA. Said he wanted to lose himself and that's what he did.

DELLA. People can't just vanish. You must have heard from him.

NOLA. Not a dicky bird.

DELLA. I bet he'll turn up again. You watch, he'll come back.

NOLA. Trevor knows how to look after himself.

DELLA. You think so?

NOLA. Course he does.

Pause.

DELLA. I never gave you up. They made you wards of court. Wanted to take you away. That's why we were in Dorset. We weren't on holiday. We were on the run.

NOLA (*pleasantly surprised*). No!

DELLA. I wasn't going to give you up without a fight, was I? We went from one holiday park to the next in Big Trevor's battered old Mini.

NOLA. I remember that car.

DELLA. We used to call it Little Nola.

NOLA. Wow! We were proper fugitives. Me and you on the run from the law.

DELLA. And little Trevor.

NOLA. Like Thelma and Louise.

DELLA. I kept hold of you for two weeks before they caught up with me. I loved my kids. We were a tight little unit.

NOLA. I knew it. Everyone thinks you were just some junkie who didn't give a fuck about her kids, but I knew you was different.

DELLA. Who said that about me?

NOLA. No one. That's what people think though, ennit?

DELLA. You're so beautiful.

NOLA. Shut up.

DELLA. You are. How did me and Trevor make something as gorgeous as you? All grown up and with a kid of your own. What's her name?

NOLA. Della. Little Della.

Pause. DELLA is visibly moved. She turns away and puts something in the box.

It's a family tradition to name the first girl after its gran. Just like you named me after a battered old Mini.

They both laugh.

Ent you gonna give me a hug?

They hug, tentatively at first then hold on to each other tightly.

DELLA. I'll give her a big kiss when she wakes up.

NOLA. She'll be asleep for hours yet.

DELLA. Am I dreaming this?

NOLA. It's real, Della.

DELLA. Because I've been here enough times in my sleep. Holding on to you so tight thinking I'll never lose you again then waking up with my arms empty.

NOLA breaks away from DELLA, *holds her at arm's length and looks at her.*

NOLA. You're even prettier than I imagined.

DELLA. Come off it.

NOLA. And you're clean now?

DELLA. A year.

NOLA. That's amazing. Do you go to them meetings?

DELLA. I certainly do.

NOLA. You got a sponsor?

DELLA. I do everything she tells me. Rebellious old me taking orders. I trust her. She's been there done it – been clean for twenty years now. When I first met her I called her the Dragon Lady. She was like a sergeant major – told me what time to wake up, when to eat, when to look for a job. I hated her. But then she tells her story in a meeting: 'Hi. I'm Vanessa and I'm an addict.' Dead posh. But her story ain't posh. Her story's the same as mine – she's a gutter addict. Lost everything, just like me. And I can't believe that this businesswoman – smartly dressed, Louboutin heels – is telling the truth. But why would she lie about it? So, I reckoned she knew a thing or two about staying well, and I stopped doing things my way and took her advice. It's working so far. How do you know about sponsors an' that?

NOLA. Julie's got one. Do you still get the urge to use? Julie does. Comes knocking on my door in the middle of the night cos she's terrified she won't be able to resist calling her dealer.

DELLA. Tell me about it. Sometimes every molecule of my body craves it.

NOLA. What do you do when that happens?

DELLA. I take a deep breath and see how long I can hold it. Times I've nearly passed out. I'm a silly cow, en I?

NANA NOLA (*calling, off*). Della! Della!

DELLA. What's the matter, Mother?

NANA NOLA (*off*). Who you got in there?

DELLA. No one.

NANA NOLA (*off*). Liar. I can hear you. You got some bloke in there?

DELLA. It's the telly, Mum.

NANA NOLA (*off*). You watching *Strictly Come Dancing* without me?

DELLA. It's the news.

NANA NOLA (*off*). Turn it over. We're missing *Strictly Come Dancing*. Come and gimme a hand.

DELLA (*shouts*). I'm making the lunch, Mum. I'll bring it through in a bit.

NANA NOLA (*off*). You said that half hour ago. You got someone in there?

DELLA. I told you there's no one here, Mum.

NANA NOLA (*off*). Liar.

NOLA. Nana Nola.

DELLA. You'd better go. She gets anxious with strangers.

NOLA. I wanna see her.

DELLA. She's not very well.

NOLA. What's wrong with her?

DELLA. Bad heart. Bad legs. Worse memory. Sometimes she's sharp as a button. Other times she don't know where she is. What do you remember of her?

NOLA. Not much.

DELLA. She used to be a right character, didn't she? Used to help out on the flower stall up the market, remember? Everybody round here knew her. You can imagine how she felt about me: 'You're a bad 'un' she used to say and I'd laugh in her face. She kicked me out when you lot left. Acted like she only had one child. You remember Auntie Marilyn?

NOLA. Vaguely.

DELLA. She's done well for herself. The big house, car, nice husband. They don't want for money that lot. One time I was at King's Cross, I see these two women come towards me. They were walking arm in arm and had their heads thrown back laughing. So, I went up to them: 'Please, miss, can you spare some change?' And guess what? – it was Marilyn out on a girly shopping trip with one of her mates. At first she didn't even look at me – just grabbed hold of her bags as though she thought I was gonna mug her. But then she looks up and sees me. Only she doesn't see me. Looks right through me. Doesn't even realise it's her own sister.

NOLA. Sounds like a right snob. You're better off.

DELLA. That's all behind me now. Never look back.

NANA NOLA *enters using a walking stick. She is wearing a sequinned gown with fluffy slippers. It is a great struggle for her to move. She stands in the doorway.*

NANA NOLA. You seen my old mum in here?

DELLA. Can't say I have. (*Under her breath to* NOLA.) She's been dead past thirty years.

NANA NOLA. She was sat on the end of my bed singing 'The Cliffs of Dooneen'. Bloody racket.

She flops into an armchair, wheezing, and takes a moment to catch her breath.

What's this then? We got guests?

DELLA. It's Nola, Mum.

NANA NOLA. Who?

DELLA. Nola. Your granddaughter.

NANA NOLA. Didn't you bring her round here yesterday?

DELLA. We haven't seen her for years, Mum.

NANA NOLA. She did. She come round yesterday with her baby. (*Addressing* NOLA.) You did, didn't you? You brought the baby round to see me. What's its name again? Nola, that's it. Little Nola and I'm Big Nola.

NOLA. No, I'm Little Nola. The baby's called Little Della.

NANA NOLA. Are you trying to confuse me? I thought you was Della.

NOLA. She thinks I'm you.

DELLA (*loud whisper*). Play along with her.

NOLA. You what?

DELLA *nudges* NOLA.

That's right. She's Little Nola. Just like you.

NANA NOLA (*to* NOLA). Now, I've told you, girl, and I'll tell you again: now you've had another kid I don't want no more of this messing around. You understand? You've got responsibilities. And I don't want you hanging around with that crowd any more. I know you think they're smart but they're a bad lot. And I don't want any of that funny business. Not under this roof. Think I don't know what you're up to? You've got the kid to think about now. And I don't want you assuming that just because you're staying here with me that I'm going to provide a twenty-four-hour babysitting service, because I'm not. Not any more. One child was bad enough, but I draw the line at two. Do I make myself clear?

DELLA *pokes* NOLA.

NOLA. Yes.

NANA NOLA. I can't hear you.

DELLA (*loud whisper, prompting*). Yes, Mum.

NOLA. Yes, Mum.

NANA NOLA. As long as we understand each other. (*To* DELLA.) You gonna give me that glass of wine, Marilyn?

DELLA. The doctor said you're to avoid booze and fags.

NANA NOLA. He don't mind pumping me full of drugs though, does he?

DELLA. Those are to keep your heart strong.

NANA NOLA. My heart's strong enough as it is. The life I've had and it's still going full pelt. I'm dying for a nice glass of wine. Where's that bottle you had?

DELLA. We agreed we'd give it away, remember? Why put temptation in front of us? I'll make you a nice cup of tea.

NANA NOLA. I've just had one, haven't I?

DELLA. You can have another one.

NANA NOLA. Only if there's biscuits.

DELLA. I got your favourites. (*To* NOLA.) She's addicted to custard creams.

NANA NOLA. You're ever so kind to me, Marilyn.

DELLA. It's Della, Mum.

NANA NOLA. Who?

DELLA. Marilyn lives in Ireland with her husband.

NANA NOLA. Oh yes. Oh, God. I thought you was Marilyn.

DELLA. If only. I'll get you a nice cup of tea. It'll make you feel better. Then I'll cook you dinner and we'll watch *Strictly* together.

NANA NOLA. Stop treating me like I'm some old madwoman. Just out of rehab and you think you've got the right to come here to my flat and take over.

DELLA. I'm here to take care of you, Mum.

NANA NOLA. Care for me? You can't even care for yourself. (*To* NOLA.) She comes out of rehab and she's got no job, nowhere to stay. She can't go back to being a prostitute, can she?

DELLA (*embarrassed*). Mum.

NANA NOLA. This is the easy option. (*To* DELLA.) I've got no money here, you know. I don't leave my savings books lying around any more. (*To* NOLA.) I wish she'd sort herself out. At least have a wash. (*To* DELLA.) You're stinking the place out!

DELLA (*patient, unflustered*). Remember what I told you, Mum, about taking deep breaths?

NANA NOLA (*confused*). What? (*As though coming to.*) Why isn't the telly on?

DELLA. Because it's rude to watch television when you've got guests.

NANA NOLA. Guests or no guests, I ain't missing *Strictly*. Ain't you getting dressed?

DELLA. I'm still tidying up, Mum. We've got hours yet.

NANA NOLA. Who's this?

DELLA. It's Nola. Your granddaughter. She's come to see us. Isn't that wonderful? And she's had a baby. Your great-granddaughter. Little Nola – she's named her after you.

NANA NOLA. Oh, that's lovely. Me a great-grandmum?

DELLA. No one would think it – you seem far too young, don't you?

NANA NOLA. Let's have a look then.

DELLA. She's sleeping, Nole.

NOLA. I'll wake her for a feed in a minute. Then you can say hello.

DELLA (*to* NOLA). You'll have something, won't you?

NANA NOLA. That's it. Get her a cup of tea.

DELLA. You don't drink milk though, do yer? You're allergic.

NOLA (*moved*). You remember.

DELLA (*tender*). So, what d'you want? Black coffee?

NOLA. Two sugars.

DELLA *leaves the room*.

You look beautiful, Nana.

NANA NOLA. Ain't you putting on a dress?

NOLA. Not today.

NANA NOLA. I don't understand you girls. Why don't you
want to dress properly? Always in jeans. Della used to have a
safety pin through her nose. It was so bloody ugly. Do you
fancy a drink?

NOLA. Della's getting us a cup of tea.

NANA NOLA (*laughing*). Tea!

NANA NOLA *gets up slowly and puts her hand down the
back of the sofa and pulls out a bottle of sherry. She sits
again then unscrews the bottle and pours some liquid into
the cap and knocks it back. She then pours another and gives
it to* NOLA, *who drinks and hands back the cap.* NANA
NOLA *pours herself another, drinks then screws the cap
back onto the bottle, which she then hides in the sofa.*

You can't leave anything out. She'll steal it. I'm telling you,
Marilyn, I'm at my wits' end. I have to watch my bag or
she'll dip her hands in my purse. And she's so bloody clever.
She takes just enough that you can't be sure she's taken anything. The other night I'm scratching my head going 'I was
sure I had a fiver in here.' And she's sitting there like butter
wouldn't melt. I've even had to put a lock on the fridge. It's
got even worse since the kids went. I hear her moving
around the house all night. She never sleeps. It's like living
with a bloody vampire.

NOLA. Maybe she's upset.

NANA NOLA. Only thing that upsets her is when she can't get
hold of her drugs.

NOLA. Maybe her heart's broken because they took her kids
away.

NANA NOLA. Heartbroken? You're a soft touch. She could always pull the wool over your eyes. Well, you don't have to live with her, do you?

NOLA. She loved them kids.

NANA NOLA. Only thing she loves is her drugs.

NOLA. Why do you talk about her like that? Like she's nothing.

NANA NOLA. You got to be firm with people like that, or she'll take advantage.

NOLA. Treat her like she's the lowest of the low? I'm not having it.

NANA NOLA. Who are you? You're not Marilyn.

NOLA. I'm Nola. The kid what got taken?

NANA NOLA. I… I don't remember.

NOLA. Oh, I think you do.

NANA NOLA. Go away. You're not real. You're just another one of them ghosts, ent you? Come to point the finger, just like all the others. They should thank me for what I done.

NOLA. What did you do, Nana?

NANA NOLA. I only saved their lives, didn't I?

NOLA. What do you mean?

NANA NOLA. When we caught up with them in Dorset, they were festering in their own filth. The little girl looked as though she had third-degree burns, the eczema was so thick on her cos madam fed her milk when she wasn't supposed to. And madam herself? Where was she? High as a tower block tooting on that bloody what d'yer call it? Pipe. That's it.

NOLA. You saying it was you had us taken away?

NANA NOLA. I didn't say nothing.

NOLA. Do you know what you done to me?

NANA NOLA. Della! Della!

NOLA. Why didn't you help her? (*Kicks box.*) Why didn't you look after me? (*Kicks boxes.*) You evil old bitch.

NOLA *kicks off, kicking at boxes in a rage.*

NANA NOLA. Della! Help! Somebody help me!

DELLA *comes running into the room.* NOLA *stops, stands panting.*

DELLA. What's wrong?

NANA NOLA. Can you see it? Over there? There's nothing there, is there? I'm the only one who can see it.

DELLA. See what?

NANA NOLA. The ghost.

DELLA. It's Nola, Mum. Your granddaughter.

NANA NOLA. She wants her revenge on me.

DELLA. She's your granddaughter. Little Nola. (*Difficult to say, but proud.*) My daughter. Imagine that. All them years gone by and she still remembers us.

NANA NOLA. That's not your daughter.

DELLA. That's not very nice, is it? She's made all this effort to come and see us.

NANA NOLA. She don't even look real.

DELLA. She's grown up, Mum. You're tired. Come and have a nap.

NANA NOLA. I don't need a nap.

DELLA. I'm taking you into the bedroom, okay? You'll feel better after a nice rest.

NANA NOLA. You're not going to leave me on me own, are you?

DELLA. Course not. I'm going to be right here when you wake up.

NANA NOLA (*to* DELLA). You're such a good daughter, Marilyn. What would I do without you?

DELLA *takes* NANA NOLA *off.*

Alone, NOLA *sits in a chair with her head in her hands. She gets up and looks into the pram. Then walks to the sofa and picks up the sequinned dress.* DELLA *comes back into the room.*

DELLA. She gets unsettled when there's new people around. She thought you were a ghost.

NOLA (*referring to the dress*). This yours?

DELLA. Don't laugh.

NOLA. Why don't you put it on?

DELLA. It's far too early.

NOLA. Go on. I wanna see you.

DELLA. You wanna make fun of me.

NOLA. I shoulda brought a dress. I look good in dresses.

DELLA. I can lend you one if you like. You can stay for dinner and watch it with us.

NOLA. I don't know how you put up with that. All those names she called you.

DELLA. She can't help it.

NOLA. Doesn't it upset you?

DELLA. Sometimes.

NOLA. So why do you tolerate it?

DELLA. I can't do anything about it, can I? She's not well.

NOLA. Do you think you deserve to be punished?

DELLA. I better get the tea on.

NOLA. She said it was her had us taken away.

DELLA. It was all a long time ago.

NOLA. You never even put up a fight, did you? Because you didn't fucking care.

DELLA. Never look back – that's what Vanessa says.

NOLA. Maybe I am a ghost.

DELLA. Don't be silly.

NOLA. What if I told you Nola died four years ago?

DELLA. That's not funny.

NOLA. Telling me. You think death is easy?

DELLA. You're no ghost.

NOLA. You wouldn't know if she was alive or dead, would you?

DELLA. I know why you're saying this and I don't blame you.

NOLA. What if I told you I wasn't Nola? What if I'm her friend Julie playing one of her tricks? Would you be able to tell the difference? Maybe I met your daughter in care. Maybe we were best friends and she told me all about you. We look alike, don't we?

DELLA. You never was in care. You were adopted.

NOLA. How do you know? What if they couldn't find a family to place her with? Anything could have happened. For all you know she could be out stone cold in some gutter right now, choking on her own vomit.

DELLA. I know it's you, Nola.

NOLA. How? How do you know? Whose nose is this? Whose eyes? You don't know because you were so out of it most of your life that you'll never be able to remember what she even looked like.

DELLA. I should know my own daughter.

NOLA. You should, shouldn't you? Oh, what's the point?

She walks to the pram and prepares to leave.

DELLA. Don't go. Please. I got so much to tell you.

NOLA. It's too late.

DELLA. It is you though, isn't it? Stop playing games and tell me it's you.

NOLA. You tell me: who the fuck am I?

Pause. DELLA *can't answer.*

NOLA *goes to the pram.*

DELLA. Let me hold the baby. Just this once. Please.

NOLA *steps aside.* DELLA *reaches into the pram and takes out the baby, holds it close until it unravels, a bundle of rags in her hands, which she allows to fall to the floor.* NOLA *quickly scoops up the rags and pushes them into the pram.*

NOLA. Ghosts. (*Laughs.*)

DELLA. Come and see me again? Promise?

NOLA *wheels the pram out and goes. Alone,* DELLA *lets out a cry. She paces the floor, restlessly. Suddenly she reaches down the back of the sofa and retrieves the bottle. She opens it and pours it into one of the teacups. She lifts the teacup and sniffs. The smell alone is intoxicating, reminding her of the sweet oblivion she used to experience in her using days.*

NANA NOLA (*off*). Della! Della!

DELLA (*puts the glass down*). Yes, Mum?

NANA NOLA (*off*). Are you still there?

DELLA. Yes, I'm still here.

NANA NOLA (*off*). I thought you'd gone and left me all alone.

DELLA. I wouldn't do that, Mum. Never.

DELLA *contemplates the teacup. She pours the alcohol back into the bottle and returns the bottle to its hiding place, then changes her mind and gets it out again.*

The End.

DANCING BEARS

Sam Holcroft

Characters

AARON, *teenager, male*

DEAN / RAZOR KAY, *teenager, male / teenager, female*

RETARD / CHARITY, *teenager, male / teenager, female*

ANGRY / BABYMOTHER, *teenager, male / teenager, female*

Three of the four actors will play both a male and female.

Setting

The stage floor is a bed of hot coals. The characters firewalk across the coals, stepping from foot to foot to distribute the pain. Different behaviours alleviate or aggravate the pain; sometimes the pain is acute, sometimes so subtle as to be almost imperceptible.

The floor is alive with red-hot coals.

AARON *emerges out of the dark. He wears tracksuit trousers and a sweatshirt covering his head with its hood pulled up. He treads across the coals. It is clear they burn his feet through his shoes. He shuffles from foot to foot to distribute the pain. But his enthusiasm for football distracts from the pain.*

AARON. The problem with the English is their lack of cooperation: instead of passing to each other, yeah, they hold the ball. I don't know whether it's the love of football that makes them see nothing but the football, or whether it's something to do with the way we learn in schools. Because, like, in Brazil, even before you get to school, even if you don't never go to school, you'll be playing football on the streets as kids. But it's different, it's called Futsal there, and it's not so much about rules and tactics, team shape, yeah, but ball skills. It's about technique. And most of these kids don't even have any shoes, but from the time they can walk barefoot they're playing on the concrete, on the tarmac, on the beaches, with no boundaries, no regulations, just ball skills: dribbling, shooting, tackling, passing – spontaneous, creative...

AARON *searches for words.*

... effortless football. In Brazil, they say that football is a dance and that the ball is your partner. In England they say that football is a game lasting ninety minutes and in the end the Germans win.

DEAN *emerges out of the dark. He too wears tracksuit trousers and a hooded sweatshirt. He eats chicken nuggets from a carton. He too struggles to walk on the hot coals. He moves from foot to foot.*

DEAN. Yeah, but we got passion.

AARON. What's the point of passion if you can't control it with your feet? In all of the World Cup, only one true striker's goal.

DEAN *raises a chicken nugget in salutation.*

DEAN. Arjen Robben's left boot against Slovakia.

AARON. No, I'm talking England here: Jermain Defoe.

RETARD *emerges from the dark. He walks hunched over, crippled with self-consciousness and malnourishment. He moves from foot to foot in dull agony, always with a close eye on* DEAN'*s chicken nuggets.*

DEAN. Tiny little Defoe.

AARON. England Slovenia.

RETARD (*chuckles*). Tiny, little…

DEAN. That was a good goal.

AARON. This is what I'm saying. Rooney, yeah?

RETARD. Roooney!

DEAN. Where the fuck was Rooney?

AARON. Centrefield, chasing for the ball. Rooney shouldn't be centre-fucking-field.

DEAN. He's a striker.

AARON. He's a striker, he should be running to the box *without* the ball.

DEAN. Without it.

AARON. Knowing someone will deliver just as he's –

DEAN *and* AARON. – in place to score.

DEAN. Yeah.

RETARD. Yeah.

AARON. Centre-fucking-field. We didn't stand a chance.

DEAN. Yeah, you knew we stopped trying to score when we took off Rooney and put on Heskey.

AARON. Fucking Heskey.

RETARD *laughs.* ANGRY *emerges out of the dark; he is twisted with aggressive energy.*

ANGRY. Fucking donkey!

The boys move as a group.

RETARD (*sniggering*). Donkey…

AARON. Seven goals in fifty-seven matches.

ANGRY. There's goalkeeper's scored more goals than fucking Heskey!

DEAN. We had our moments, though. John Terry's fish dive!

AARON. That's what you want centre back. Someone willing to put their brain between the ball and the goal.

DEAN. That's some instinct.

AARON. No, instinctively you'd put your hands out to protect you, but he dives for it, arms by his sides, like a, like a eel or something.

DEAN. Yeah, like a eel.

They all imitate John Terry, diving headlong for the ball like a wriggling eel.

ANGRY. Like a eel!

RETARD. Like a eel!

AARON. That was commitment!

They laugh and show off for each other. RETARD accidentally stumbles into ANGRY. ANGRY turns on him in a fit of malicious violence. He smacks him, beats him back, holds him fast and steals his shoes. Barefoot on the coals, RETARD mews in agony. He tries to hold his feet in his hands but his hands burn on the coals. ANGRY puts on RETARD's shoes over his own. RETARD tucks his feet into the ends of his tracksuit, he moves from foot to foot in quiet agony. DEAN and AARON begin to feel the pain of the coals more keenly.

DEAN. Our boys sure got passion.

AARON. Yeah, but what about technique? The Brazilians, the Argentinians, the Portuguese are carving up the grass with not so much ball control, but *mind* control that was learnt them way back when they had no shoes and the hot ground was burning through the soles of their feet. But they weren't feeling it because of the game.

DEAN *struggles to cope with the pain of the coals.*

DEAN. The beautiful game.

AARON. Villa, Xavi, Ronaldo.

DEAN. Kaká.

AARON. Better than Kaká, better even than Torres... the best in the world today –

DEAN. No contest.

AARON. – Lionel Messi.

DEAN. Small and fast as lightning.

AARON. Like he's doing the Riverdance and the ball is on a string tied to his toe. Did you know his father was a factory worker and his mother a cleaner?

DEAN *steps from foot to foot, the agony visible on his face.*

DEAN. Uh-huh.

AARON. My mum was a cleaner when she was working.

DEAN. We know.

AARON. He joined his local football club when he was five.

DEAN *unscrews the cap on a bottle of vodka and takes a drink. It alleviates the pain.*

DEAN. And you joined yours when you were seven.

AARON. So he had two years on me.

DEAN. But you'll make it up.

DEAN *offers the bottle to* AARON.

AARON (*shaking his head in refusal*). His father was coach of the club; they went to practice together every week. I bet they even practised when they come home.

DEAN. I bet they did. Drink, why don't you.

AARON. Passing up the garden and scoring across a goalpost made from chairs or something.

ANGRY and RETARD eye the bottle of vodka hungrily. They step from foot to foot in pain.

DEAN. Tastes good, Aaron.

AARON. And his mother would come home and cook for them cos they'd be tired after training.

DEAN. What an angel.

AARON. Yes, an angel. Cos when he's fifteen, he's diagnosed with a hormone deficiency.

DEAN feigns surprise, he's heard all this before.

Yes, some growth hormone or something – which is why he's so small.

DEAN. But fast as lightning!

AARON. She could've said, she could have said, 'We can't afford the hormones *and* the training, so you is just going to have to work the factory like your father.'

DEAN. Just a little, Aaron.

AARON. But instead…

DEAN. Just a little bit.

AARON. Instead they up and moved their entire lives so he could train for Barcelona and they paid his medical bills.

DEAN. A little makes all the difference.

AARON. Because she loved him so much.

DEAN. Aaron.

AARON. Because she gave up everything for him, he will go down in history maybe as the man whose legend outlives Diego Maradona's! Football boots got studs; they raise you off the ground.

The pain in AARON's *feet gets the better of him, he begins to twist in discomfort.*

DEAN (*nodding towards the bottle*). That'll send you sky high.

AARON. If I drink I can't practise.

ANGRY. Let me have it then.

DEAN *puts a hand out to stop* ANGRY.

DEAN (*to* AARON). Course you can.

AARON. No, I can't miss another practice. Last time my mum, she couldn't even get out of bed. I couldn't leave her.

DEAN. Can't practise if you're anxious neither.

AARON *looks at the bottle of vodka.*

Can you?

AARON *takes a swig from the bottle. It dulls the pain.* DEAN *smiles.*

See, that was easy.

ANGRY. Let me have it now!

AARON *takes another drink and passes the bottle to* ANGRY, *who drinks heavily.* DEAN *puts his hands flat on the coals.*

DEAN. Look, it don't burn no more, does it?

See? Nothing!

ANGRY *laughs. The bottle passes to* RETARD, *who drinks and puts his hands on the coals just like* DEAN; *he grins.* ANGRY *tears across the coals in delight.* DEAN *does a cartwheel. Even* AARON *gets caught up in the excitement. They pass around the bottle of vodka and lose themselves to this dreamlike world without pain.*

RETARD. Hey! Hey, look at this!

RETARD *picks up a red-hot coal and eats it; he gnashes his teeth and snarls and laughs manically.* ANGRY *picks up some crushed coals and stuffs them down his pants and grabs his groin. The others laugh and cheer.*

ANGRY. You know I was telling you that this girl was breathing like really...

ANGRY *imitates shallow breathing and rubs his groin.*

...cos of the cock in her mouth. And the other guy's in and out her arse so hard that blood comes running down, and her eyes – she's like staring, with this expression...

The others stagger with inebriation, engrossed in ANGRY*'s story.*

...like I once saw a picture of a monkey, a research monkey, with a hole in the top of its head and it was like that, like that look in its eye, like, like... fuuuuck! You know?

They nod and laugh.

And I was like concentrating so hard, I mean I was only eleven or something, I hadn't seen it before, I was concentrating so hard – (*Mimes tipping his plate.*) that my spaghetti fell off onto the carpet and my mum was like, 'Don't fucking throw your spaghetti on the carpet, you little fuck!' And then my dad was like, 'Keep it the fuck down, I'm trying to watch the fucking movie.'

They laugh hysterically; the laughter dies away. The bottle empties, they catch their breath; they begin to sober up. They look at their burns. They blow on their skin.

ANGRY *clutches his groin and groans in shock.*

Fuck, fuck...

RETARD *puts his finger to his mouth; his mouth is full of blood. He whimpers pathetically and turns to* DEAN *in agony.*

DEAN. It's alright. No problem, it's alright.

RETARD. Ow...

DEAN. Who wants my last chicken nugget?

ANGRY. Fuck your chicken nugget.

DEAN (*to* RETARD). You want it? Don't you?

DEAN *offers the chicken nugget to* RETARD. RETARD *looks at it with incredulity.*

Your mum might call you 'Retard', but you're not stupid, are you?

DEAN *nods in encouragement and proffers the nugget again.* RETARD *takes it.*

That's it. Smart man.

DEAN *and* RETARD *smile at each other. It eases the pain. In a fit of jealousy,* ANGRY *tears across the coals and twists* RETARD*'s arm behind his back;* RETARD *squeals in agony, but holds the chicken nugget aloft.*

(*To* ANGRY.) That's enough.

RETARD *yelps in pain and tries to eat the chicken nugget.*

You're a soldier, aren't you? Aren't you my soldier?

ANGRY. Yeah, I'm a soldier.

DEAN. Well, soldiers don't get their high from thieving.

ANGRY *releases* RETARD. RETARD *twists in pain and begins to remove his sweatshirt.*

AARON *turns to leave.*

(*To* AARON.) Where you going?

AARON. Practice. I've got to go while I can. Last time I couldn't leave my sister. I told her, I said, 'Charity, don't try and carry Mum upstairs on your own.' But she doesn't listen. And I come home and she's sprained her wrist.

RETARD *has removed his sweatshirt, underneath he wears a tight-fitting top, revealing the feminine curves of her body, she moves like a woman.* ANGRY *and* DEAN *turn to stare at her as she moves from foot to foot with all the innocence and femininity of a fifteen-year-old girl. She is* AARON*'s little sister,* CHARITY.

CHARITY. Where you going?

CHARITY *steps from foot to foot in pain.*

AARON. Practice. They're going to stop picking me and I won't go up for trials. Imagine if Lionel Messi –

CHARITY. I wish you'd stop talking about fucking Lionel Messi.

AARON. Don't curse, Charity. If Lionel Messi had let something get in his way, then football wouldn't be the beautiful game. I got to get to practice.

CHARITY. Aaron?

AARON. What, Charity?

CHARITY. I was in a car at the traffic lights and I saw across the other side of the road a baby fox.

AARON. I don't have time, I have to –

CHARITY. It had run out from someone's front garden and it was so tiny it could hardly walk on its little legs.

AARON. Charity, please.

AARON *turns to go*.

CHARITY. But it bounded across the pavement like Bambi and ran into the road just as the lights changed and the car in front took off.

AARON *stops*.

And my heart, like, jumped into my throat all of a sudden but the car stopped and I thought, 'Thank God, it's stopped just in time,' and I was waiting for it to run out the other side but I couldn't see it and then the car in front swerved and drove around it and I could see that it was still running, the baby fox, but running on its side with his head now facing its tail and blood coming from its mouth with these wild, wild eyes. And though I only saw it for a second I can't stop seeing the image in my mind. And when we drove past again on the way back it had gone, but there was a stain on the tarmac, like someone had been sick.

AARON. I've got to go.

CHARITY. No.

CHARITY has fashioned RETARD's sweatshirt into the shape of a baby.

I can't watch him for you no more.

CHARITY places the baby in AARON's arms. CHARITY turns to DEAN, she beams at him with love.

DEAN (*to* CHARITY). Fox cub. That's the name for a baby fox – fox cub.

CHARITY. No, that's a bear cub.

DEAN. Yeah, and fox cub. It's the same.

CHARITY. Isn't it a puppy?

DEAN. What?

CHARITY. Fox is more like a dog than a bear.

DEAN (*laughing*). No, it's a fox cub, it's not fox puppy.

CHARITY. Well, I like baby fox. I can say that, can't I?

DEAN. You can say what you like.

CHARITY. Then I will.

They look at one another; they smile.

Don't you think it's funny, Dean, that you can say 'baby fox, baby bear, baby bird,' but you don't say 'baby human'.

DEAN. You say 'human baby'.

CHARITY. Yeah, but you don't go saying, 'Oh look at that lovely human baby,' do you? Human baby's just a baby, isn't it?

DEAN. You're beautiful.

CHARITY smiles.

I can't do nothing but look at you.

CHARITY. I can't do nothing but look at you.

They embrace. They lie down and roll together; taking it in turns to lift each other off the coals.

ANGRY *watches them with growing longing and hunger.*

As DEAN *and* CHARITY *roll together,* AARON *searches in earnest. He cradles the baby.*

AARON. It's alright. It's alright, little man.

AARON *darts about with the baby in his arms, the baby cries louder.*

I know, I know, but I can't find it, can I? Where the fuck is it? Charity?

CHARITY *steps in time with* DEAN *and stares at him adoringly.*

How can I find it in all this shit? Charity!

CHARITY. What?

AARON. Help me.

CHARITY. What's the matter?

AARON. I can't find it.

CHARITY. What?

AARON. I can't find his shoe.

CHARITY. Find it later.

AARON. Can't find it later; late already. He was supposed to be back with his mother an hour ago. Charity!

CHARITY. Alright!

CHARITY *breaks away from* DEAN *and helps* AARON *look for the shoe.* DEAN *and* ANGRY *step in time together, hoods pulled low over their heads.* ANGRY *continues to watch* CHARITY *with lustful curiosity.*

Dean is buying me dinner.

AARON. Where's she put it?

CHARITY. An Italian restaurant.

AARON. Where's Mum left it, huh?

CHARITY. He's so… generous. Tells me I'm the only girl in every room I walk into.

AARON (*looking for the shoe*). Come on, where are you?

CHARITY. Every compliment lights me up.

AARON. I can't keep track of everything.

CHARITY. I feel I'd do anything for a –

AARON (*checking the time*). Fuck.

CHARITY. – compliment.

AARON. Fuck!

CHARITY. See, I don't care about the restaurants.

AARON. I don't have time.

CHARITY. Don't care about the money.

AARON. I'll have to…

CHARITY. It's the praise: it's a drug.

AARON. …leave without it.

CHARITY. I love him.

> AARON *trips, the baby screams,* CHARITY *steadies him.*

> Careful! What's it matter?

DEAN. Charity?

CHARITY. It's just a shoe.

DEAN. I'm short on cash, Charity.

> AARON *shrugs her off and trudges away across the coals, cradling the baby.*

> CHARITY *turns to* DEAN *with love.*

> (*Referring to* ANGRY.) Go with him up the High Street and fleece as much as you can, yeah?

CHARITY (*with a smile*). Why's that now?

DEAN. No one's going to suspect you cos you're so beautiful.

CHARITY. Yeah, I think them shops owe a little… Charity.

DEAN (*nodding*). You know you're my best girl.

CHARITY *beams at him.* DEAN *nods to* ANGRY *and treads away across the coals.* CHARITY *steps in time with* ANGRY. *He touches her; she swats him away.*

CHARITY. Hands off.

ANGRY (*touching her again*). It's your body should be illegal.

CHARITY. Hands off me. (*Pushing him back.*) Get your stinking hands away from me or Dean will cut your throat.

ANGRY. That right?

CHARITY. Yes.

ANGRY. I'm his soldier.

CHARITY. I'm his best girl.

ANGRY. His 'best girl'.

CHARITY. That's right.

ANGRY. What does his 'best girl' do for him?

CHARITY. 'Do for him'?

ANGRY. If I get close I'll probably smell it.

CHARITY. I said get off.

ANGRY. But unless your pussy offers protection then I outrank you.

   ANGRY *begins to grope her.*

CHARITY. Dean?

ANGRY. I'd put my brain between a bullet and him; I offer that commitment.

CHARITY. Dean!

   DEAN *treads calmly back across the coals towards them.*

ANGRY. Where do you think he'd be without me?

DEAN. S'alright, Charity.

CHARITY. Tell him to get his hands off.

DEAN. Relax. It's okay; he's only playing.

CHARITY. Dean?

ANGRY *runs his hands over her.*

DEAN. We're just playing a game.

AARON *talks to his baby –*

AARON. It was a good game, little man!

CHARITY. You said…

AARON. A really good game.

DEAN. You don't know, Charity, cos nobody showed you.

CHARITY. You said that you loved me.

DEAN. But this is what love is: compromise.

CHARITY. 'Compromise'?

AARON. I'm getting better every time.

DEAN. Yes, a real relationship we're having here.

AARON. I really think this could be it.

DEAN. Don't you want a real relationship?

CHARITY *slowly nods.* DEAN *smiles.*

That's right. Good girl.

Together, DEAN *and* ANGRY *grope and molest her; their actions become increasingly violent.* AARON *continues to entertain his baby…*

AARON. I stormed up the side, see, running faster with the ball than the rest could without it and I cut in up top and scored on my left boot. My left boot! And guess what, you'll never guess, turns out there was a football scout in the stalls. And he come up to me after and says I got 'an obvious talent'. Did you hear that, little man? 'An obvious talent'! He wants me to try out for his Youth Team. D'you know what that means? That's the break I been waiting for, my opportunity to go professional. I'm gonna be a professional football player and they earn, like, sick amounts of money.

As AARON *dances in elation with his child,* ANGRY *and*
DEAN *reach a climax in their sexual frenzy over* CHARITY.
After writhing with pleasure, ANGRY *steps back from*
CHARITY *and stretches in relief. As he does, he unzips his*
sweatshirt to reveal feminine curves underneath. ANGRY
now moves with all the femininity and weariness of teenage
mother, BABYMOTHER.

We're gonna be rich, little man!

BABYMOTHER. Give him to me.

CHARITY *picks up the discarded sweatshirt and stumbles*
away; she holds her crotch and steps from foot to foot in
agony.

AARON (*laughing, dancing with his baby*). You hear that…

BABYMOTHER. Don't hold him like that.

AARON…. We're gonna be so fucking rich!

BABYMOTHER. You're late.

AARON *turns to* BABYMOTHER.

I was thinking all these thoughts!

AARON. Nothing happened.

BABYMOTHER. I didn't know what happened, I don't know
where you are.

AARON. I was just…

BABYMOTHER. Who you're with. I don't know which tramp
is holding my baby.

AARON. I was holding him.

BABYMOTHER. You ask me to take you seriously and you
can't even get him home on time.

BABYMOTHER *examines the baby.*

AARON. I was at practice. I had such a good –

BABYMOTHER. Practice.

AARON. Yes.

BABYMOTHER. So where did you leave our son?

AARON. Home.

BABYMOTHER. I don't want him in your house, I told you.

AARON. What was I supposed to do?

BABYMOTHER. Where's his shoe?

AARON. I…

BABYMOTHER. Aaron?

AARON. I don't know.

BABYMOTHER. You lost it?

AARON. My mum, she…

BABYMOTHER. Are you fucking joking, you dickhead? I told you not to leave him with your mum. Now I've got to buy another fucking pair of shoes.

AARON. I'll buy them.

CHARITY *uses* ANGRY*'s discarded sweatshirt to stuff her belly in pregnancy. She approaches* DEAN. DEAN *ignores her.*

CHARITY. Dean?

BABYMOTHER. Do you know even how much they cost?

CHARITY. Look at me, Dean.

AARON. If I get selected for the Youth Team, I can start paying more.

BABYMOTHER. I don't want to hear it; I don't want to hear any more about the team.

CHARITY. Dean, what's the matter, please?

BABYMOTHER. Just go, I don't want to hear it, don't want to see you. Go!

AARON *turns away, frustrated and distressed. He kicks the coals, the sparks burn his calves; he twists in pain.* DEAN *blocks* AARON*'s path.*

DEAN (*to* AARON). Where you going, Aaron?

AARON. I got trials for the Youth Team.

DEAN. Youth Team?

AARON. Yeah.

DEAN. And what when you get in this Youth Team? More practise? Practise every day? That's quite a commitment. John Terry'd be proud.

AARON *forces another uneasy smile; he tries to walk on. Once again* DEAN *stops him.*

What about us? What about your commitment to us?

CHARITY. You don't say nothing nice to me.

AARON. I make time, Dean, but what with the baby and –

DEAN. Youth Team, yeah. Think about your baby, Aaron, family's important.

CHARITY. You won't even look at me?

DEAN (*to* AARON). You're not going to turn your back on the family, are you?

AARON *holds* DEAN*'s gaze before treading across the coals, away to practice.* DEAN *watches him go.* CHARITY *reaches out to touch him again; he pushes her away.*

CHARITY. What?

DEAN (*pointing to her pregnant belly*). I don't even know whose it is.

CHARITY. You, Dean.

DEAN. I don't know that. I don't know how many people you fucked.

CHARITY. But, you…

DEAN. How are we supposed to know who put it there?

CHARITY. Dean, please...

DEAN. Don't come crawling to me cos you gave your self-respect to any dick that poked you. You're no different from your mother.

BABYMOTHER. I used to have some sick thoughts, you know?

DEAN. Fucking men on the stairs while your children eat their tea.

CHARITY. No, Dean.

BABYMOTHER. Sick kind of suicidal thoughts.

DEAN. The apple don't fall far, does it?

CHARITY. Dean!

DEAN *pushes* CHARITY *away; she stumbles across the coals towards* BABYMOTHER. BABYMOTHER *screws on the lid of a baby's bottle. She talks to* CHARITY.

BABYMOTHER. I used to want to know what a bullet feels like.

BABYMOTHER *tests the temperature of the milk on her arm.*

I kind of welcomed it. I never thought of it as suicide, but that's what it was, I guess. Wanting to die.

BABYMOTHER *takes* CHARITY*'s arm and squeezes milk onto her skin to show her the right temperature. They both step from foot to foot to distribute the pain.*

I didn't care about living, didn't have nothing to live for.

CHARITY *nods and licks the milk off her arm.*

Till now.

BABYMOTHER *cradles the baby and feeds him the bottle.*
CHARITY *watches.*

Just me and him now.

CHARITY. Aaron is trying.

BABYMOTHER. Don't rely on them.

BABYMOTHER *offers her the baby;* CHARITY *shrinks back with alarm.*

You can only ever trust yourself.

BABYMOTHER *places the baby in* CHARITY's *arms, helps her to position the bottle. She nods in encouragement.*

Telling you they love you, telling you they'll come through for you, that they can make a hundred thousand pound a day just kicking a ball along the grass.

CHARITY *feeds the baby; she looks at him with wonder.*

Don't count on it. Otherwise you'll be waiting all your life. I'd still be in that house with seven people in them two rooms. Eight people when my uncle come to stay. And when I found blood in the nappy, I knew I had to get out.

CHARITY *looks up at* BABYMOTHER.

You can only ever trust yourself. Get on the waiting list now, it took me eleven months.

CHARITY *looks back at the baby.* BABYMOTHER *smiles encouragingly.*

See? It's easy.

Together, CHARITY *and* BABYMOTHER *step in time and rock the baby.*

AARON. Charity! Charity?

The two girls look up: AARON *races across the coals towards them.*

BABYMOTHER. Shhh, you'll disturb the baby.

AARON. You'll never believe it!

BABYMOTHER. Keep your voice down.

AARON. I got selected.

CHARITY. What?

AARON. You are looking at the newest recruit for the Youth Team. I made it.

CHARITY. Are you being serious?

AARON. Yes, I made the team! I am going to play professional football. I get a salary, sponsorship, everything, and I get a football shirt and boots, with studs that raise you off the ground!

CHARITY. Aaron, that's amazing!

CHARITY *leaps up and throws her arms around his neck. AARON swings her round and they squeal in delight. AARON sets CHARITY back on the coals; he looks at BABYMOTHER.*

BABYMOTHER. Is it true?

AARON *nods. He produces a new pair of tiny shoes; he offers them to her. DEAN approaches. BABYMOTHER looks at the shoes, she smiles.*

DEAN. Congratulations.

They all turn to DEAN.

You made the team. The *team*. You are so... clever. You've done it again. Again you manage to convince someone that you're a *team player*. What will they do, what will they do, Aaron, when, like me, they realise you used their trust to make fools of them? When you walk the moment there's a better offer?

AARON. Dean, I...

DEAN. You are an artist of manipulation, my friend, cos you had me thinking we was family.

CHARITY. He's doing this for us; we're his family.

DEAN. Was I talking to you?

BABYMOTHER. He's got a son to raise.

DEAN. Since when does a whore speak over me?

BABYMOTHER. Don't you call me a whore.

DEAN (*to* AARON). Keep your baby-factory out of our business. Or I will.

AARON steps between DEAN and the girls.

AARON. Hey, come on...

DEAN continues to goad AARON.

DEAN. I should've known.

AARON. Dean, this doesn't have to be –

DEAN. I should've known I couldn't trust the two of you. Your mother never taught you no loyalty. You was a wasted investment.

AARON. Dean, this doesn't have to –

DEAN. You want out, you got to fight your way out.

DEAN beckons AARON.

CHARITY. No, Aaron!

The two boys launch themselves at each other. They struggle across the coals, hot ash and sparks spray up around them. The girls scream and watch helplessly. They grapple with each other desperately, until AARON overpowers DEAN and pushes him down onto the coals. In a moment of recon- ciliation, AARON extends a hand to DEAN to help him up. As he does, DEAN produces a knife and slashes AARON's Achilles tendons. AARON yells in agony and clutches his ankles; he falls onto the coals, he writhes in pain. CHARITY runs to his side. DEAN backs away, wild-eyed, and unzips his sweatshirt to reveal a feminine physique; she moves with self-confidence; she is RAZOR KAY. She steps from foot to foot on the hot coals.

RAZOR KAY. Mum never washed my clothes so I guess I stank. The teacher washed my shirt and tights in her own home, but it didn't make no difference. So, one day, I brought a razor blade into school and when they cornered me outside the dinner hut I whipped it out and held it at one of their necks and actually pricked some blood. Since then I always carry one with me, you know, make me feel safe. Once it went too far though and it got me expelled. I had to go to a special school. But my reputation, you know, they knew my reputation. And they was even more up for a fight there. I used to keep one under my tongue. And I could, like, spit it out and hold it between my teeth and cut like that, you know...

RAZOR KAY *slicing with a razor blade between her teeth.*

That's how they call me Razor Kay. I get a rush out of it, it's like, like sugar, drink, drugs – addictive, can't get enough. There was this one girl walking towards me and she had this really nice handbag and diamanté iPhone and I just hit her in the face with a plank of wood. I think I took out her eye.

BABYMOTHER *eyes her nervously.*

So who is it you want beating?

BABYMOTHER. My uncle.

RAZOR KAY *waits for an explanation.*

They took away my mum's house and so I said she could come and live with me. I came down this morning and he was there, she'd let him in. I don't want him coming round the house no more.

RAZOR KAY *nods in agreement.* BABYMOTHER *kneels on the ground and offers her body to* RAZOR KAY *as a stool in thanks; she grits her teeth against the pain.* RAZOR KAY *sits on her back and raises her feet off the ground in relief. When they stand the two girls step from foot to foot in synch.*

CHARITY *approaches* BABYMOTHER.

CHARITY. You said you could only ever trust yourself.

BABYMOTHER. I said you couldn't trust no men. And I've got to think of my baby. You've got to think of yours.

CHARITY. Yeah, but your uncle's a big man.

RAZOR KAY. I ain't afraid of that, I been hit that many times I can't remember.

CHARITY. You been shot, though?

RAZOR KAY. Shot at. Gun up against my forehead then pistol-whipped and put in the back of a car.

BABYMOTHER. Fuck.

RAZOR KAY. Know what I mean? And I'm sitting in the back of the car and this bitch is laughing, her tits are shaking though her top –

RAZOR KAY *laughs.*

She's laughing so hard cos she thinks she, you know, she thinks she's caught the big fish, isn't it? But she doesn't realise I got a razor blade under my tongue and I've spit it out and I'm cutting her up the arm and face before she even can feel it and there's blood everywhere.

BABYMOTHER. No!

RAZOR KAY *(laughs).* And they opened the door and pushed me out, I was rolling over in the road. They never come for me again, that's for sure.

BABYMOTHER *laughs.*

BABYMOTHER. When Aaron and I was together and this girl would come sniffing round him, I crushed her glasses, so she couldn't even see.

RAZOR KAY. That's nothing. This one girl was always hanging round my man, he was only into her for her money, so one day I, like, put a knife to her back and made her go to the cashpoint, you know, and take out the maximum amount. At three different banks. And then I made her go with me shopping for clothes with the cash and I was like 'Do you think he'd like me in this?' And then I said she could earn the rest back by doing a striptease, you know, and I'd put the money in her G-string.

RAZOR KAY *laughs. The others look at her, unnerved.*

Come on, I ain't no dyke. I don't get off on that. She was just some stupid bitch needed to earn her daddy's money, is all.

BABYMOTHER *and* CHARITY *look at each other.*

I love the cock, alright. I love big, hard, pulsating fucking cock.

The other two laugh.

You love the cock, right?

BABYMOTHER. I love the cock.

CHARITY *laughs.*

RAZOR KAY. Charity?

CHARITY *points at her pregnant belly.*

CHARITY. Does it look like I fucking love the cock or not?

RAZOR KAY (*laughing*). Yeah…

The girls laugh together.

CHARITY. I ain't doing their work no more. They got nothing I need that make it worth it.

BABYMOTHER. No, sir. Me neither.

CHARITY. I ain't thieving for them no more. I'm doing it for me. Look…

CHARITY *pulls three bracelets of the same colour out of her pocket.*

I took these. Three. I thought they was beautiful.

She holds up the bracelets for the others to see.

They may be stronger than us, but a razor cuts through muscle, right?

RAZOR KAY. That's right.

CHARITY. By ourselves, we can do this. We can do anything they can do, so long as we stick together.

CHARITY *offers the bracelets to the other girls. They take the bracelets and slip them over their wrists. They touch them with pride. They smile.*

RAZOR KAY *moves towards* CHARITY *and lifts her off the coals.* CHARITY *stretches in relief. They take turns to lift each other and begin to move in synch. Many of their unified movements mirror those of the boys at the beginning of the play. The more they band together the less they feel the pain. Soon they feel nothing but love for each other.*

RAZOR KAY. When this girl had her thumb in the corner of my eye.

BABYMOTHER. I had you.

RAZOR KAY. You jumped in and beat her.

CHARITY. I held her.

RAZOR KAY. We are family. You are my sisters. Family would die for each other. I'd die for you.

BABYMOTHER. Just so long as you don't want to fuck me, then that's alright.

RAZOR KAY. We don't fuck unless we want to.

BABYMOTHER. No.

RAZOR KAY. We don't love unless we want to.

CHARITY. Never.

RAZOR KAY. We don't do nothing for no one but each other.

BABYMOTHER. That's right.

RAZOR KAY. They may be stronger than us one-on-one, but together we can tie them up –

CHARITY. Yes.

RAZOR KAY. – take their money –

BABYMOTHER. Yes.

RAZOR KAY *produces a gun.*

RAZOR KAY. – and stick their gun up their arsehole!

RAZOR KAY *wields the gun aloft.*

You don't get more liberated than that.

CHARITY *and* BABYMOTHER *stare at the gun in awe.*

BABYMOTHER *approaches and* RAZOR KAY *allows her to inspect the gun.* CHARITY *approaches* AARON.

CHARITY *is so consumed by love for her girlfriends that she feels little pain in her feet.*

CHARITY. Razor wants to buy us all trainers, you know, in the colour to match the bracelet. So everywhere we walk, people know we belong to each other.

AARON *is silent; he trembles.*

I told her not to spend her money; see, I don't care about the money. I'd tie a purple rag around my arm. It's the loyalty: I can't get enough. We're like kids in a sweet shop.

CHARITY *smiles,* AARON *stares into the distance.*

RAZOR KAY. Charity?

CHARITY. It's love.

AARON *looks at* CHARITY *in alarm.*

RAZOR KAY. Charity?

CHARITY *turns to* RAZOR KAY *with a smile.*

CHARITY. Yes, Razor.

RAZOR KAY *offers the gun.*

RAZOR KAY. I want you to carry it for me.

CHARITY. What?

RAZOR KAY. I want you to carry it until I need it.

CHARITY. But –

RAZOR KAY. Because you're my best girl.

BABYMOTHER. Razor?

RAZOR KAY *puts an arm out to silence* BABYMOTHER. BABYMOTHER *stares in jealous indignation.*

RAZOR KAY. Nobody is going to suspect you because you're so lovely. You're so lovely, Charity. You're like my little sister. I'd die for my little sister. Will you carry this for me?

CHARITY *nods, tentatively she takes the gun.*

That's right, good girl.

CHARITY *feels the weight of the gun.*

Sometimes, some people, they don't listen to nothing but the barrel of a gun, yeah. It don't matter how big your uncle is, how strong he is, all you got to do, Charity, is point it – (*She mimes cocking the gun.*) and we'll take care of the rest.

CHARITY *stands with the gun. She turns to* AARON.

CHARITY. Aaron? Aaron, I have this fantasy that I'm holding a gun… up against Dean. And he, he's shrinking like a violet cos all he's got is a knife. (*Laughs.*) What you gonna do with that knife, Dean, I'm all the way over here? By the time you get to me I'm gonna shoot that knife right out of your hand. So that you know I'm being serious.

CHARITY *points the gun at an imaginary* DEAN.

And when you're frozen like a bunny rabbit in my headlight, my sisters are going to creep up on you and beat you…

RAZOR KAY *and* BABYMOTHER *mime beating a man to the ground.*

…in your arms, your legs, your chest, your throat, till you lying on the ground and dying slowly. Maybe so slowly that I give birth before you go, and I hold up my child and show you your own face reflected. The last thing you ever see!

Aaron?

CHARITY *cocks the gun.*

Aaron, do you dare me?

The sound of a police siren explodes through the space, CHARITY *jumps in fright. She tosses the gun away and raises her hands above her head.*

BABYMOTHER. You idiot!

RAZOR KAY. What did you tell them?

CHARITY. I was only carrying.

BABYMOTHER. Is you a grass now?

CHARITY. I carry between neighbourhoods, but I don't sell. That's all I said.

BABYMOTHER. I knew you shouldn't have given it to her.

CHARITY. I dropped the gun, didn't I? They didn't even know about that.

BABYMOTHER. So now we don't even have a fucking gun?

CHARITY. Well, what did you want me to do, keep hold of it? I don't want to go to jail. It was the hash, okay? That's all they had to go on, and I didn't mention neither of you. Alright? Alright?

RAZOR KAY. So when you got to go to court?

CHARITY. I don't. Cos I'm a first-time offender. (*Laughs.*) So they think! They said so long as I go to some meetings then I don't get a record.

CHARITY *attempts to sound blasé.*

I was like, oh alright, if I must! So all I got to do is show up, eat some biscuits, yeah, and my record stays as white as snow.

CHARITY *laughs.*

RAZOR KAY. That going to take a lot of time?

CHARITY. What?

RAZOR KAY. That's quite a commitment, those meetings, no?

CHARITY. I don't know.

RAZOR KAY. What about your commitment to us?

CHARITY. I am committed to you, but what with the baby and the –

RAZOR KAY. Meetings, yeah. Think about your baby, Charity. Family's important. You don't want to turn your back on the family, do you?

CHARITY *speaks to* AARON.

CHARITY (*to* AARON). While I was sitting there I was thinking to myself, praying to God: 'Please, please Lord don't send me to jail. If you spare me I'll do your work, I swear I'll be your angel on earth and I'll make amends.' And

when I come home you was asleep so I crawled into bed
with Mum. And this morning I woke up and she was looking
over me, crying, and I thought I'd died and was in the casket.

AARON *struggles to remain standing.*

The other day I watched a grown man get punched in the
face till he was basically dead, and the only thing I can't get
out my mind is a baby fox that didn't do nothing but run out
into the road. I keep seeing it, running, you know, on its side,
but it's not the running, it's not its twisted spine, it's the eyes,
Aaron, cos even though it was dying, even though its life
was beaten out of it, its eyes... its eyes were on fire.

CHARITY *moves away across the coals.* RAZOR KAY
follows her.

RAZOR KAY. Where you going? Charity, where you going?

CHARITY. I've got to go to a meeting.

RAZOR KAY. You know something, Charity, all them judges,
all them magistrates, police or whatever, they don't know
what real life is like for us.

CHARITY. I have to go, Razor.

RAZOR KAY. They don't know nothing about waking up cold
and fucking hungry with no shoes to put on your feet. They
are just looking at you like you're nothing because that's all
they know.

BABYMOTHER. Nothing.

RAZOR KAY. It's just a job for them, just ticking a box. They
don't care about who you are; they're not interested.

CHARITY (*to* RAZOR KAY). What's that?

RAZOR KAY. They just want to tick the box.

CHARITY. What is that?

RAZOR KAY. Stick with me I can tick a fucking paper.

CHARITY. What the fuck is that, Kay?

RAZOR KAY. Bullet-proof vest.

CHARITY *looks at her, incredulous.*

You got to show them that you ain't messing around. You're not a pussy; you are a warrior in your own right. You dress like one.

BABYMOTHER. That's right.

RAZOR KAY. Dress like your body was built for fighting.

CHARITY *looks at her with horror.*

(*To* BABYMOTHER.) You understand.

BABYMOTHER. Course.

RAZOR KAY. Cos you is a soldier. Aren't you my soldier?

BABYMOTHER *twists with aggressive energy.*

BABYMOTHER. That's right.

The two of them move in time; CHARITY *backs away slowly.*

RAZOR KAY. What's the matter, Charity? It was you who said we can do it if we stick together. We're just doing like you told us. Don't you want to stick with us, Charity?

CHARITY *hesitates.*

If you want to stick with us then you won't go.

CHARITY. I have to.

RAZOR KAY. No.

CHARITY. I'll get a record.

RAZOR KAY. I'd take that on for you.

CHARITY. No.

RAZOR KAY. I wouldn't think twice about it. You don't know because nobody showed you, but that's what family is, what it's all about: compromise.

CHARITY *begins to shake her head.*

Yes. Sacrifice. The sacrifices I make for you: I fight for you;
I lose teeth for you; I'd kill anyone who so much as come
near you with a bad word. It's love I'm giving you. Love in a
desert of dry hearts.

CHARITY *backs away shaking her head.*

What do you need that I don't give you? Fuck, Charity, what
more do they offer you than that?

CHARITY *doesn't respond.*

I should've known I couldn't trust you. Your mother never
taught you no loyalty. What will they do, what will they do,
Charity, when like me they realise you turn your back on
them just as soon as there's a better offer?

CHARITY *turns away from them.*

If you want to leave, you have to ask nicely.

CHARITY *ignores her.*

Where are your manners, Charity?

CHARITY *tries to get away from them; they pursue her.*

Don't be rude, you know how it is: if you want to be excused
you have to ask nicely. Ask me nicely.

RAZOR KAY *takes a razor blade out and artfully weaves it
between her fingers.*

Come back and thank me, show some politeness, Charity!
All the things I did for you, you so easily forget? The people
that hurt you, I marked their faces so they wouldn't forget
what they did to you. Come back, get down on your knees in
front of me and beg me to mark you so that every day you
look in the mirror and see me, so you don't forget me. So
you don't never forget me.

Both RAZOR KAY *and* BABYMOTHER *set upon*
CHARITY. *They grapple with her across the coals.*
CHARITY *manages to knock the razor blade out of* RAZOR
KAY*'s hand, but even so they drag her face down onto the
ground and push her belly into the hot coals, she wails in
pain. They hold her still.*

BABYMOTHER *and* RAZOR KAY *back away, they put on their sweatshirts, pull up their hoods and leave.* AARON *hobbles towards* CHARITY; *he rolls her onto her back. He pulls the sweatshirt out of her T-shirt. Her pregnancy dissolves in his hands. He helps her to sit.*

CHARITY. Aaron... I...

AARON. Shhh, it's alright. Here, here, up you get.

AARON *helps her to stand.*

There you go.

CHARITY. Aaron?

AARON. You know what?

CHARITY. What?

AARON. The problem with the English is their lack of cooperation.

CHARITY. Aaron...

AARON. I'm telling you, instead of passing to each other, yeah, they hold the ball.

AARON *dusts her down.*

But see in Brazil, even before you get to school, even if you don't never go to school, you be playing football on the streets as kids. And most of these kids don't even have any shoes, and the hot ground is burning through the soles of their feet.

AARON *guides* CHARITY *away. They step in time together. Hobbling from foot to foot.*

But they not feeling it because of the game, you know? The beautiful, beautiful game...

Together they disappear into the dark.

The End.

THAT ALMOST UNNAMEABLE LUST

Rebecca Lenkiewicz

Characters

KATHERINE, *a prisoner, lifer, seventy, slight, northern*
LIZ, *a prisoner, lifer, fifty, robust, from Norfolk*
A SINGER/ A WRITER, *twenty-five, from London*

Setting

The action takes place in a prison and in the minds of Katherine and Liz. Katherine and Liz's cells should be inhabited and quietly kept alive by them whilst other actions are going on so that we have a sense of them spending constant time in their respective cells. Their cells might be suggested simply by a floor plan created by yellow tape which delineates realistic dimensions of a modern prison. The room might be the same, yellow lines that suggest walls… or a crime scene.

Scene One

A space.

Night. A SINGER *stands at a microphone, a flower in her hair. She mouths the words to a 1940's version of a man singing 'You Always Hurt the One You Love' ... A glitter ball lights the room.* LIZ *and* KATHERINE *dance, by themselves, within their cells, but as though they had partners, late-night, close, but to no one.*

Scene Two

A room.

KATHERINE *sits in a chair and makes strange, almost whistling sounds through her teeth... a bird-sounding noise, hardly perceptible.*

A WRITER *walks in. And sits down.*

WRITER. Katherine?

    KATHERINE *stares at her.*

Your Support Officer said that you might want to talk to me. Outside of the group. He said that you often write. And that you might want to show me some of your work. He said that you can talk but you... prefer not to. Is that right?

    KATHERINE *nods.*

The WRITER *hands* KATHERINE *a pad and pencil.*

If you'd rather...

    KATHERINE *takes it and does nothing with it.*

Does it hurt... Katherine? When you speak?

No reply. KATHERINE *stares at the* WRITER.

But you can hear me?

KATHERINE *nods. She makes the bird sound again.*

Scene Three

The garden.

LIZ *kneels down. She weeds and takes dead leaves off a plant.*

LIZ. You want some more light there, don't you?

She looks up towards the sky, inspects the shadows.

No. That's your lot. You won't have no more today.

Scene Four

Katherine's cell.

Sounds of metal doors. KATHERINE *sits alone. She takes a cigarette out of a pack. Considers it. Counts in her head and checks how many are in the pack. She puts the cigarette back in the pack, perturbed that she has miscounted. The lights go out sharply.*

Scene Five

A room.

KATHERINE *and* LIZ *sit in a circle with six other women who are represented by chairs. A* WRITER *leads a workshop. The* WRITER *waits for* LIZ *to introduce herself...*

LIZ. Liz...

WRITER. Yes... but with an animal. Like Lou just did. Lou... lizard. You say your name with an animal so that we can remember it better.

LIZ *looks around the circle,* LIZ *and* KATHERINE *have a moment, undecided.* LIZ *can start a revolt and diminish the* WRITER *or not. She smiles. Slaps her knees.*

LIZ. Liz... tiger...

WRITER. Great... and...

It is KATHERINE's *turn.* LIZ *nods, waits. The* WRITER *looks at her notes.*

Katherine... something with a K?

Gina says, Ku Klux Klan.

LIZ. You're soft, Gina. The Ku Klux Klan isn't an animal.

WRITER. No... Katherine?

KATHERINE *looks at her, can't speak.* LIZ *nods... waits.*

LIZ. Katie... kitten.

WRITER. Good. If that's fine with you, Katherine?

KATHERINE *looks down at the floor, cannot reply, she instinctively makes the bird sound. The* WRITER *feels awkward.*

Are you... alright?

LIZ *watches* KATHERINE, *then puts her hand on* KATHERINE's *knee.*

LIZ. Bless you, Katie. Bless you...

So you gonna send us this book when you've written it, are you?

The WRITER *is still worried about* KATHERINE.

She's alright. Katie's grand.

WRITER. Yes. I will.

LIZ *nods, unsure of whether the* WRITER *will.*

So... grab a pen, everyone... and write this down. 'The Place.'

LIZ *and* KATHERINE *take up a pen and paper.*

LIZ. Why do you presume I can write?

WRITER....Sorry... I... Stupid of me... If you dictate... I'll write it for you.

LIZ. I can write. I just don't think you should assume that everyone can.

WRITER. Oh... I see... So is there anyone else who can't write?

LIZ. You're not listening to me. I can write.

WRITER. Is there anyone who can't? No... Okay, so... pen, paper... I want you to write down a place where you were happy... maybe from your childhood. A happy time.

LIZ *and* KATHERINE *look at each other, both aware of the other's harsh childhood.* LIZ *smiles, shakes her head. The* WRITER *picks up on this but is resilient.*

Just... any happy time. It doesn't have to be when you were young. Write down where and when. You were happy.

LIZ *and* KATHERINE *stare, thinking. Their pens do not move.*

Lou? Any thoughts? Doesn't matter if you've written
nothing down. Katherine?

A beat. KATHERINE *looks at her. Makes the whistling
sound.*

LIZ. Thinking's as important as writing. Gestation period.

WRITER. It is.

LIZ. Tell me something... My thoughts... sometimes they go so
fast that if I wrote them down, the speed they come out, the
paper would catch light. Eh? How would you describe that
then? When it's flying fast between your head and the paper?
Like fireworks?

WRITER. Does it feel like you're getting something off your
chest? A catharsis maybe...?

LIZ. No. It's never that.

An electronic bell sounds.

WRITER. Is it... a release?

LIZ. Free-flow.

WRITER. Yes... maybe... like free association.

LIZ. No. It's free-flow now. Between the buildings. We have to
go.

WRITER. Oh. Thank you all. For your time.

LIZ. One thing we got plenty of.

WRITER. I hope to see you again.

LIZ. We're not going anywhere. Katie?

LIZ *and* KATHERINE *stand and leave and go back to their
cells.*

Scene Six

Katherine's cell. KATHERINE *sits alone. When speaking to herself her speech is fluid but when talking to others it verges on stammering as she finds it so difficult.*

KATHERINE. The Place… is hundreds of miles north of here. It is mountains. Rain. Mist. Everance. White lichen. Scorching sunshine. Green slopes with grey scree scars. Frogs of all patterns, some the size of your thumbnail. Red deer. Grouse. Granite sparkling. Wood gnarled and bleached. As silver as Christmas spray-paint with the way the light hits it.

There are no walls. No smell of disinfectant. No small windows…

In the prison canteen the younger ones jump the queue. I watched a woman bent over her food. The two girls at her table talk, heads bent in to each other. She cries. Quietly. Into her mashed potato. Then eats it. The girls do not notice.

Scene Seven

Liz's cell.

LIZ. In a garden you can't do anything too… strident. Even watering. If you water them when it's sunny their leaves will scorch. Peaceful out there. Apart from the people.

Scene Eight

Katherine's cell. Liz's cell.

They are in their separate spaces.

KATHERINE. The writer asked us, 'What do you miss? Do you miss… men?' 'No,' we shouted. All of us. Except for Gina. Gina's a compulsive liar. Gina's a natural irritant. Which is ironic as her life's mission is to please. Which in itself is of course innately… irritating. She has come-to-bed eyes combined with a little-girl-lost. In a fifty-five-year-old that is not appealing.

All I remember of my marriage was the need to get away. A proposal would be like catching a train. When I married I had to hold my flowers permanently in front of me. A farce. A lot of misguided fumbling. Not very clever.

I miss colour. In people's faces. Lou is a greyish shade. Her teeth look as though you could simply pluck them out from her gums… Prison skin. Almost translucent. A human jellyfish because she has hit the outside air so seldom. I miss sweeps of colour. Swathes of sky. And sea. I miss turning my head from left to right following the horizon. Nothing here is on an epic scale. Even a person's footsteps seems to diminish in size.

LIZ. What is sweetest about the garden is that things change. Brown earth one day and a green shoot the next. A tiny spear. Unstoppable.

KATHERINE. When you empty a deer's stomach at noon it is full to bursting with vivid shredded grass. It's a huge viscous veined balloon. The innards are greyish violet. Pa would cut the throat to drain the blood. A gully of deep red pours out. He pulls out a purplish tube from the hole, cuts it, scrapes it, knots it. Yanks out the windpipe. A muscular tube the width of a child's arm.

LIZ. I don't miss men. Aisha, she had a fella started writing to her. Muslim chap. A year on they arranged to marry. Never met or laid eyes on each other. Didn't see each other for the actual service. Some postal union. Something. She still had two years left in here. They met finally. In the visiting room. 'What'll I do?' she said to me. 'They won't let you do very much,' I said. 'Let him do the talking. It's him who's done the chasing.' She went in and sat down, all made up. He walked straight past her at her table. Then he went back to her and sat down. Couldn't look at her. She couldn't look at him. Newlyweds, staring in different directions. This carries on for a minute. Then he takes her hand. He still doesn't look at her. He stares at her wedding ring. He says, 'That's nice.' And then he drops her hand and walks out. My marriage weren't much better. Knew him, of course. Didn't know he was cruel. More than cruel. Forced me to do... all sorts.

KATHERINE. Pa holds the back legs apart. He stands there above the deer looking at it. Looking at me. Then he sinks the knife in and cuts from the pubis to the front legs. His hands reach in. Disappear.

LIZ. Bodies. Complicated. I never got it. How God designed us. There's too much mismatch. You look at flowers. Butterflies. Minor birds. Every detail, every colour amazing... But an old woman wandering around a bus station swearing, skin a mass of sores, with her life in bags... You can't call that a perfect creation, can you?

KATHERINE. He chucks out the spleen, small, flat, dark. Then he pulls out the huge double stomach. It slaps out, full. He runs his knife down it like a zip. Green belches out. It's as if he were emptying a lawnmower. He unravels the intestines as though he's playing cat's cradle. Pa's hands are covered in blood. He washes the tripe in the rain pool and throws it to our dog Joey.

LIZ. Fear's a terrible thing. The sweat of it. The repetition of it.

KATHERINE. I see large droppings right under the deer's tail. The beast rolled down a hill after Pa shot it in the head. Was it conscious then, whilst hurtling down the hill? Or was this an after-death spasm? And suddenly my fascination turned to utter sadness. Pa picks up tufts of sphagnum and cleans his hands with it. Squeezing the water from the moss.

LIZ. They say, some people, they half-strangle each other for
pleasure. That pressure to the windpipe can be exciting.
Arousing… I didn't find that to be the case.

KATHERINE. We sat and ate with the stag behind us. All shit
and guts. I looked back and there were bubbles of blood
coming out of its nostrils. A jelly just below them. Wasps had
already invaded its mouth. Perfect teeth. Pale tongue. I
turned away and I hugged my legs.

LIZ. I watched a film he'd left in the machine. He didn't care
what I found. Pictures. Magazines. Used tissues. Terribly sad,
the film was. Some young girl covered in… she didn't look
much older than fifteen. Not what you want to see. I slept
next to him that night, I cried hard into my pillow. Cried for
that little girl with her face… I don't care if she was smiling
or making cash. Her business. Live and let live. But she was
so beautiful and they were so… not. Some of the girls here,
they never stop feeling each other up in the canteen. Hands
under T-shirts. Tongues as far as they'll go. Harmless. But
when I really think about it, it's circus tricks. Grasping. It's
not touch. Real touch. When that happens you don't want
people around to witness it. Too private. Too… perfect.

KATHERINE. I touched the antlers which were grey and furry.
Velvet under the fingers. 'Bad head,' Pa said, 'Not enough
points on the horns.' I wanted to stroke its muzzle and say,
'Good head. You're perfect.' An eyeball hung out which
looked far too big for its socket. But the other eye shone the
most perfect violet. Up at the sky.

LIZ. He had a routine. Most nights. Pub till closing time. Come
back. Drink. Vocals. Objects. Then me. He'd work himself up
to it. He'd say 'Why are you so… big? Wouldn't it be lovely,'
he'd say, 'To be with a woman who would bend over for me
and I'd not be repulsed? It's not asking for much, is it?'

KATHERINE. 'Mum's locked the door,' I would say. 'She's
inside but she won't let me in.' And so I'd trail around with
Pa.

LIZ. When you're trapped. You stay. You… submit. Maybe
somewhere else exists but probably it doesn't. It's like being

underwater. No fast moves. No struggling. And then you find ways of numbing the pain. And each pill is a tiny brick you build around yourself. The tiniest of walls but still it confines you. Defines you. And then you're ill as well as static.

KATHERINE. I used to run a lot as a girl. Here I try not to let my steps become smaller. Lou has become geisha in her confinement. She shuffles along. Not helped by the tracksuit that always slips beneath her stomach. Mermaid scars on her sagging pale belly. Stretch marks from the four children she has borne.

KATHERINE *walks around her cell.* LIZ *walks around hers. The* SINGER *sings 'You Always Hurt the One You Love'.* KATHERINE *and* LIZ *dance to it, alone in their cells, very defined by the rectangle of it. They dance as though they have partners but they do not.*

Scene Nine

A room.

The WRITER *talks to* KATHERINE, LIZ *and the six other women.* LIZ *is restless and spikier than we have seen her before.*

WRITER. Gina, you can put your hand down.

LIZ. Put your… flying hand down, will you, Gina? How many times does she have to tell you?

WRITER. It doesn't matter. Just… It's not school. So what did you want to say…?

Gina pauses… cannot remember what she wanted to say.

That's fine, maybe you'll remember it in a bit.

LIZ. Saints preserve us.

WRITER. Okay… So… the Prophet Muhammad was running away from some persecutors. And he hid in a cave and his friend said, 'This is crazy, we'll be found here.'

LIZ. Is this a joke?

WRITER. No no. It's a story. So, Muhammad's in the cave.
And Allah, he wanted to protect the Prophet so he created
cobwebs and made trees grow so that nobody would see the
entrance or realise that the cave was inhabited. Because it
was so concealed. And I just wondered if any of you felt a bit
like that? That you related to that? Gina, you don't need to
put your hand up.

LIZ. She thinks she's a prophet. That's why she's got her hand
up.

WRITER. What was it you wanted to say, Gina…?

Again she has forgotten.

Okay, you have a think.

LIZ. You say Muhammad was protected. These walls… it's
not… we're not. It's like plants if you don't give them
drainage. They rot. Stagnate.

WRITER. Do any of you feel you've benefited from prison in
any way…? No. But Gina, you said you felt it had given you
time.

LIZ (*to Gina*). You'll say anything you think the other person
wants to hear… Yes you will. And then you say stuff about
us. Which isn't true.

WRITER. Okay… Let's go back to this idea of time. Lou, you
said you felt prison had sort of punctuated your life.

LIZ. Yeah. Given it a big fucking major fucking full stop.

WRITER. You think it's a mad idea, Liz? That prison might
give some women just time on their own. To break patterns.
Aisha?

LIZ. And start new ones. Like drug dependency. Clinical
depression. Self-harm. Smoking. You can't get through
prison without fags. You just can't.

WRITER. I suppose it's comfort, yeah?

LIZ. No. You're not listening to me. It's not comfort. It's
necessity.

WRITER. Are you okay, Liz?

LIZ. No, no. Actually. No, I'm not alright. You're talking about some prophet in a cave. And you're very nice and your book'll have a shiny cover. WH Smith and all that. Picture of you on the back drinking… coffee. But I don't think you quite realise what this place is. It's a hole. A big black fucking hole. Lou's granddaughter died, didn't she, Lou? Four years old. At the funeral, Lou was cuffed to the guard and not allowed to talk to anyone. What did they think she was going to do? So she couldn't speak to her daughter or hold her when she was going through all that hell… Sorry, Lou, I know it upsets you…

Lou nods, saying how hard it was.

Exactly. Humiliating. Harsh. Her daughter's child dies. And she's chained like a dog in the fucking church. Now, Lou may be many things. A junkie… sorry, Lou, but you know… but she is not dangerous. Actually, probably I'd say you could count on two hands how many women in this prison are a danger to society. Now, you can say we need to be punished. Fine. But we're not fucking dangerous. And we're not fucking lunatic. Most of us, anyway.

WRITER. Right. Okay.

LIZ. No no. You see, you use these words and they mean nothing. 'Right. Okay.' It's all pacifiers. You say write about trees you've sat under. Write about boats you've been on. Dresses you've worn. You come in here with your 'Start a sentence with "If I ruled the world"…' If I fucking ruled the world, I'd shoot every fucker in it. Why don't you ask me to write about the sound of my nose breaking? Or my ribs cracking? Why do you avoid that?

WRITER. I didn't want to… impose.

LIZ. Quite fucking right too. Probably time you got off our patch, really. Fuck off with your fucking prophet.

WRITER. I'm sorry. I thought you were enjoying the sessions.

LIZ. You keep saying, 'What do you feel, Liz? What's going on in there?' I tell you I smile. I talk to you. But inside I'm screaming. Every minute. Do you see that?

The WRITER *says nothing. Does nothing.* KATHERINE
puts her hand on LIZ*'s knee, takes her hand.*

Thanks, Katie… Sorry. I… didn't take no pill this morning.
Thought I'd try and do without it. Fucking birthdays…

Lou asks, is it Liz's birthday? LIZ *gathers herself.*

No, it's not mine. Couldn't give a flying fuck if it was mine.
No, it's Clara's. Yeah, my youngest. Her thirtieth today.

Lou says, she's sorry, it's not easy.

She took my coming in here hardest, you know? Couldn't
talk to me for a long time. She's got friends, though. All over
the place. Friends.

LIZ *breaks down now, tries to cover it but can't, and*
KATHERINE *puts her arm around her.* LIZ *turns herself to*
KATHERINE *to hide herself from the others. The* WRITER
watches.

Go away. Please.

The WRITER *stays a moment too long then leaves.* LIZ *cries*
and KATHERINE *makes her strange whistling sound and*
pats LIZ*'s back, holds her.*

Sorry, Katie. I'm sorry… I'll be alright in a bit.

KATHERINE *talks but it is in her mind.* LIZ *calms into*
stillness.

KATHERINE. I have an image of each of the women here. But
   outside. You, Liz… with your thick plait and your ruddy
   cheeks… You're the farmer's giant wife. Outside a farm-
   house peeling potatoes. Shouting at the chickens. You ride a
   tractor. Green wellies. Then you go in and knead bread on a
   huge kitchen table. Flour on your fringe and the radio is on.
   There are Border collies in a hayrick that run riot whenever a
   visitor appears. Your legs are furrows in fields. Later, you let
   your hair down and you bathe naked in a river, watched by a
   lonely gamesman in the forest. He longs to call out to you.
   To tell you that your beautiful body stops his heart. That he
   can't sleep for thinking of it. That he aches for you to sit next
   to him. Beer in hand. Watching shapes in his bonfire.

LIZ. Oh, Katie… I really let the side down, didn't I?

KATHERINE shakes her head.

Free-flow bell sounds. They get up.

Scene Ten

A room.

The WRITER *and* KATHERINE *and* LIZ *and the women sit in a circle.*

WRITER. How is everyone this week?

No huge response.

Liz? Did you get hold of your daughter? On her birthday?

The WRITER *has crossed a vivid red line.* LIZ *is outraged.*

LIZ. That was really the problem. That I couldn't 'get hold of her'.

WRITER. Sorry… I just thought you might have… rung her or something.

LIZ. Maybe you should stop speculating about our lives and tell us about yours.

WRITER. Mine? Nothing exciting. Nothing compared to here.

LIZ. You think here is exciting, do you?

WRITER. It's very… full.

LIZ shakes her head, amazed.

LIZ. You're not listening, are you?

LIZ raps on a plastic chair.

It's like that in here. Man-made. Plastic. Grey. Uncomfortable.

Gina raps on a plastic chair too.

Why do you do that, Gina? Why do you copy me like that?

(*To the* WRITER.) You want to know what I'm in here for, don't you? What I did?

WRITER. No.

LIZ. Not very curious. For a writer?

WRITER. I'd... like to know... of course I would. That's what I do... story.

LIZ. It's not story. It's real life.

WRITER. But I would never ask.

LIZ. But all the time you're thinking it... 'What did she do?' Sixteen years, it's not nicking fags from the corner shop, is it?

WRITER. Do you think you should be in here?

LIZ. I'm guilty of what I was charged with. Most of us are.

Gina has her hand up.

WRITER. Gina... you don't have to... you can just ask... or speak.

Gina says she's not guilty of her crime.

Really? That's awful. How can they do that to you?

LIZ. You can say that Gina and I know that you believe it. But you're not gonna get ten years in here for drugs without doing something... No, I know. I absolutely believe that you think that you are innocent. That is your truth. And you need that truth. Absolutely. But... no matter... forget I ever said it...

LIZ *becomes uncharacteristically awkward.*

WRITER. So. A list. Of places you would be if you were not here.

LIZ *nods, the free-flow bell sounds.*

Scene Eleven

Katherine's cell.

KATHERINE *sits.*

KATHERINE. I have a book. I have carved the pages out of it
    to make it hollow. To keep my tools in. A lot of the
    youngsters here do it. I asked the doctor about self-harm.
    Told him I had flirted with it a little during my marriage. I
    burnt a cigarette onto my hand when that seemed the only
    thing to do. And one night I banged my head against the
    kitchen wall. And I realised that pain could be displaced.
    That it was mobile. I told him, 'When I cut myself, there's
    no pain. Only relief. And actually a bit of a rush.'
    'Endorphins,' he said. 'They're a natural painkiller.'

Dr Pi prescribed pills. I didn't take them. I preferred the
    razor.

KATHERINE *sits down on her bed.*

Scene Twelve

A room.

The WRITER *sits with* LIZ *and* KATHERINE *and the six other
prisoners.*

WRITER. How did anyone get on?

LIZ *and* KATHERINE *nod.*

Did anyone write anything?

LIZ *breathes, a touch nervous, then launches in.*

LIZ. I wrote something. But it's not, strictly speaking, 'A Field' like you said.

WRITER. Doesn't matter. Anything's great.

LIZ. Here we go. 'I looked up what he did...' Gina, I'm reading. Don't put your fucking hand up.

WRITER. Ask any questions later, Gina.

LIZ. Shall I start again? I'll start again. 'I looked up what he did. What happened with us.' Gina, fuck's sake, what can you ask about it yet? I've read two sentences.

LIZ *settles back to her piece of paper.*

'Five sort of types of violence they listed between people. The description best for what he did was called "intimate terrorism". Plus a lot of "non-reciprocal violence". Which made it sound like I wasn't much fun to play with. Which I wasn't, as it goes. Two thirds of women who were killed by their husbands had been battered first. I do know one thing. Which is the rage that I felt. The violence I did. It was only for him. I would no more hurt another person... anyone... a stranger... than I would hurt my grandson Gideon, who is six and a beautiful boy. I would die a hundred times, any manner of ways, rather than let any harm come to Gideon. I have held him in my lap a few times. But I don't want him in here again. I don't want him smelling these smells or hearing women screaming. So I shan't see him till he's older. Nothing happened very differently that night. He was no worse than usual. He kissed me goodnight. After hitting me. I looked at myself in the bathroom mirror and the light bulb had been broken in there for a while. I'd replaced it today but with a stronger watt. And when I put the light on and saw myself. My face. The colours looked so much brighter than usual. And I thought of Clara. And how he'd teased her that day. About her weight. He wouldn't stop. And she pushed her dinner away. And looked embarrassed. At her beautiful little stomach. She held it in. Wanted to cry. So that night I sent her to her auntie's. And I did it. Afterwards I couldn't move for a bit. Just looked at him. I drank bleach. Don't

know why. But at the hospital they gave me a charcoal drink.
Disgusting. Stopped the bleach from eating me alive.'

Considers the WRITER. *Looks round to the others.*

I had a bit at the end but I crossed it out. Didn't think it
was... I said, 'He hits me he hits me not.' I saw that years
ago on a poster campaign... but anyway I crossed it out.
Bit... slick.

WRITER. Right...

The WRITER *can't think of what to say. Lou says, well done,
Liz, that was very good.*

LIZ. Thanks, Lou. Thank you very much.

The free-flow bell sounds. The WRITER *leaves.*

Scene Thirteen

Katherine's cell. Liz's cell.

LIZ. Makes me nervous. Moving. Like starting a new school.
Stupid. It'll be better for Clara. Means she can get back to
Gideon, doesn't need to leave him for the night. Much better.
Talked to him on the phone the other day. 'Are you coming
down the park, Nan?' he said. 'I'm taking my bike.' 'I'll come
another time,' I said. Clara tells him I'm at the library. That's a
lot of fucking books I must have read. 'Are you rehabilitated?'
they ask. No. I'm just a lot tireder than when I came in.

KATHERINE. When I first came in, my mother came here on a
'glass visit'. I put my hand to the glass. She just looked at it.
Then she looked away.

LIZ. I can't think about getting out. No. A day at a time. That's
all I can do.

KATHERINE. The writer has left now. She has completed her
research.

LIZ. I shall miss my garden. Grew that one up. From scratch.
Watched it been dug up. Everything has happened to it over
the years. Spat on. Pissed on. Kicked. Cigarettes stubbed out
on it. Replanted it. Watched girls trying to fornicate with the
new guard behind that shed. That poor young man. Terrified,
he was. Running away from the greenhouses.

KATHERINE. Will you have your thick plait until your dying
day, Liz? Liz. Tiger.

LIZ. 'I'll miss you,' the writer said. She won't. I don't ache for
champagne. Or sex on a high-speed washing machine... I'd
like to be in a park. Watch a sunset while I'm walking. Hear
the sounds of a few youngsters kicking a ball around. Smell
of bonfires in the autumn. See a small boy. Getting off his
bike. Hold his hand.

KATHERINE *makes the whistling sound*.

KATHERINE. My father. Calling grouse. He would lure them
with that call. 'There's a fine covey,' he'd say.

KATHERINE *whistles*.

They would look at him. Why would they think that such a
big man was a chick? Such a big man. Not tall. But heavy.
Very heavy. 'Lots of people do it,' he'd say, 'but no one's
allowed to say. If you ever told your mother it would kill her.
Don't hurt her,' he'd say. And wipe his hands on the moss.

KATHERINE *remembers her father and the damage he did
her for a moment but tells us no more*.

Scene Fourteen

KATHERINE *and* LIZ *stand in the space*.

LIZ. They're ghosting me, Katie. Tomorrow.

KATHERINE *nods, takes this in*.

Didn't expect it after all this time. Come to say goodbye.

KATHERINE *and* LIZ *look at each other. They do not embrace.*

Bye, Katie. God bless you.

KATHERINE *tries to speak, she does, falteringly.*

KATHERINE. Goodbye… Liz… bless you…

LIZ *starts to walk away.* KATHERINE *shouts.*

Liz! Tiger!

LIZ *does not look back but waves goodbye with her back to* KATHERINE, *who walks to her cell, bereft. She sits on the bed.*

I am in some woods. Silver birches. The sun comes down and through them in shafts. Damp leaves. Moss. A fast but shallow river. I put my arm into it. You appear. I hide amongst the trees. And watch you bathe. In the water. Blue sky. You undo your thick hair and it falls over your shoulders and down your back. It is flax yellow against your skin… which is twelve different shades of white.

'You Always Hurt the One You Love' plays. The lights are prison neon. LIZ *dances cheek to cheek with no one in her cell.* KATHERINE *watches her.* KATHERINE *takes down her book. Takes out a razor. Gently cuts her arm. Breathes. The lights change to muted.* KATHERINE *keeps watching* LIZ. *She makes another light cut. Breathes. A glitter-ball effect happens.* KATHERINE *watches. Watches.*

Blackout.

The End.

DORIS DAY

E V Crowe

Characters

DAISY, *mid-twenties, white*
ANNA, *mid-twenties, white*

Dialogue in [square brackets] indicates intention, not to be spoken.

Late.

DAISY *in pyjamas.*

ANNA *in half-uniform.*

DAISY. I wouldn't want to do a protest.

ANNA. No.

DAISY. You were there though?

ANNA. –

DAISY. Poor you.

    Pause.

    Did you volunteer?

ANNA. They put me down for it.

DAISY. Oh right.

ANNA. Don't ask me why.

DAISY. You're tall.

    Pause.

ANNA. It wasn't just hippies…

DAISY. Okay.

ANNA. It was quite hardcore.

DAISY. Was the sofa comfy?

ANNA. Hardcore. I was right up front. I told you I got MAST-trained?

DAISY. They must think you're good! Six tequilas good.

ANNA. Got to!

    They brought a team in from Manchester.

DAISY. Why?

ANNA. Because it was *some-heavy-shit*-why.

DAISY. You know why they put you at the front?

Pause.

For the cameras. That's what they say.

ANNA. If that was the case, they'd fill the line with officers who look like someone called for a stripper. And blonde. Like you.

DAISY. I put your uniform in my cupboard.

ANNA. You know the team call you Doris-Day-Easy-Lay.

Pause.

You are! Don't get offended. That's what they say.

DAISY. MAST-trained. That's cool.

Pause.

ANNA. I'm properly surprised they didn't pull you in.

DAISY. No one trusts a transfer at a protest.

Pause.

ANNA. What you doing then?

DAISY. What?

ANNA. You out in the car? One of the cars?

DAISY. No.

ANNA. What then?

DAISY. Cell watch.

ANNA. Fuck me.

DAISY. You swear lots now you cut your hair.

Pause.

Don't you do cell watch?

ANNA. Only when the team hate me.

Silence.

I sort of wish I was working tonight. You know that feeling?
Keep-going feeling?

DAISY. What about Carl?

ANNA. This? This is us 'having a bit of space'. You know.

Pause.

DAISY. Nice face by the way.

Pause.

What happened?

ANNA. Oh some fucker fucking cunt customer mugged me on
my way back. Just now.

DAISY. Shit.

ANNA. Quite bad! It hurts.

DAISY. I just assumed it was from work.

ANNA. Did you?

DAISY. So…?

Pause.

You going to call it in?

ANNA. You haven't asked if I'm okay.

DAISY. No, no, I know. I'm just… are you okay?

ANNA. It was a – (*She illustrates a headbutt, expertly.*)

DAISY. Did you struggle?

ANNA. A bit.

DAISY. Okay.

You going to call it in?

DAISY *picks up her phone.*

ANNA. YES. It's easier not to.

DAISY *puts down the phone.*

DAISY. We won't 'tell the police'?

Pause.

ANNA. I don't want the team to find out.

DAISY. I agree. Fuck the team…

ANNA. No, it's all about the team Dipsy-daisy-woo. Wake up. The point is I had my file on me. You can't lose a fucking case file. You're not even supposed to take them home.

So don't blab. K?

It was just a mugging.

Pause.

Don't babysit me. I'll just… Can I have some of your Night Nurse?

DAISY. Top cupboard. And there's wine if you get the right mix.

Pause.

When I do get to go out in the car, Domestic Violence, DV's all I ever seem to get.

ANNA. And back to you. Is it?

DAISY. You never get called out on DV?

ANNA. Careful.

DAISY. What.

ANNA. Careful.

DAISY. Of what.

ANNA. Careful you don't start seeing DV everywhere.

DAISY. DV is everywhere. Statistically. Actually.

ANNA. TRUE!

Pause.

DAISY. Boring but true.

ANNA. DV is boring, Daisy. DV paperwork! Fuck. It was rape
you know, that gave us our 'in'. I'm not ungrateful to rape.
Thank fuck for rape. I'd do rape reports every week for a promotion, I'd ask all the funny questions –'did he touch you?'
'where did he touch you?' 'which breast, left or right?' – every
day if it got me into plain-clothes, you'd probably have taken
an actual raping to get your transfer… you know. You'd have
had to go for it, as is the nature of 'rape'. If they had raped you
for a transfer, they would have done it fucking slowly. Really
fucking slowly, because 'that's how they roll'. They'd be
raping you while you filled out the forms. So slowly. You'd be
bending over asking for a pen. So you could tick a box to say
you felt *marginalised* and yes, tick, *disempowered*.

DAISY. You seem okay. Workwise.

Pause.

ANNA. Variety isn't it?

DAISY. *You* get variety.

ANNA. I get lucky.

DAISY. Cool.

Pause.

ANNA. Cheer up.

Pause.

Cheer up. I'll say good Daisy-type-things next shift.

Pause.

Remember who saw three dead bodies!

They high-five.

DAISY. That is true. Thank you.

DAISY *goes into her room.*

ANNA *wipes some of the blood off her face. Emotional.*

DAISY *comes back in uniform.*

ANNA. You look cute.

DAISY. What?

ANNA. You look tiny.

DAISY. Okay.

ANNA. You do.

DAISY. It's because the vest doesn't fit.

ANNA. No. It's your teeny arms.

DAISY. Okay.

ANNA. I'm just going to rest.

DAISY. You should.

Pause.

So, which way did he run?

ANNA. Who?

DAISY. Your mugger.

ANNA. Towards the main road.

DAISY. Did you chase him?

ANNA. –

DAISY. Did you pursue? Go go gadget arms?

ANNA. I love chasing. I shouted. Rah!

DAISY. 'Call the police'? 'Call the police'? 'Call the police'?

Pause.

Had you ever called the police before you joined the police?
Like nine-nine-nine.

ANNA. – no.

DAISY. It's hard to call the police.

ANNA. Maybe I wasn't very loud. I scream quite quietly.

DAISY. Lucky. If you've decided you're not going to say
anything.

Pause.

ANNA. It's nice us being on the same team.

DAISY *pretend-headbutts her. Like a joke.*

DAISY *collects her things to go.*

Don't kill anyone.

DAISY. I wish.

Morning.

DAISY *in uniform.*

ANNA *in pyjamas.*

DAISY. So she's in the car…

ANNA. –

DAISY. A Citroën. She's crying.

ANNA. This is quite a shit story.

DAISY. She asks… Liam.

ANNA. I know Liam.

DAISY. …to step back a bit. So he leans in. You know how his face is. Telling her she's taking the piss with no brake light. She said he scared her how fast he drove up behind her. He's practically spitting at her now.

ANNA. Daisy, I always get spat at.

DAISY. So I told him to back off.

ANNA. In front of her?

DAISY. Yes.

ANNA. What did you say?

DAISY. I said 'Liam, back off please.'

ANNA. Could the customer hear?

DAISY. The customer wasn't down as deaf.

ANNA. What did she say?

DAISY. She was crying.

ANNA. Fucking Citroën drivers.

DAISY. I had to say something.

'Liam, back off please.'

ANNA. 'Liam, back off'?

DAISY. I had to.

Pause.

ANNA. You know we said before about not mentioning anything. If they know we're friends, from home? I'm just not sure it's a hundred per cent professional, then for them to clock that.

DAISY. Won't they be able to tell?

Pause.

ANNA. Didn't you have a friend on your last team?

DAISY. Gemma.

ANNA. Gemma. What's Gemma doing now?

DAISY. On the beat.

ANNA. How long's she been doing that?

DAISY. Three years.

ANNA. Exactly.

Day.

DAISY *in uniform.*

ANNA *in pyjamas.*

ANNA. Second sick day ever.

DAISY. Okay.

ANNA. I don't need you to tell me it's okay.

DAISY. Carl was asking around about you.

Pause.

Do you think he knows I'm a transfer?

ANNA. We're the police. Even I've read your file. Apparently you have good soft skills.

DAISY. I can talk to people.

ANNA. Funny you have a good day when I'm off.

Pause.

'Soft skills.'

DAISY. They're just other types of *skills,* as valid as some might say as being able to push something 'angry man' heavy.

Like Domestic Violence is actually still really 'Assault', except, I don't know, with mood lighting. They have a way with words don't they?

ANNA. Who?

Pause.

What about 'at early'?

DAISY. I can talk to people any time of day.

ANNA. What about 'at early' when they have a knife.

DAISY. I can talk to people.

ANNA. Good.

DAISY. I'm not interested in my…

ANNA. Arrest target? Sure.

DAISY. Liam is.

Liam keeps count.

He'll try and make an arrest before I can.

ANNA. He'll poach it?

DAISY. Liam is always, counting.

ANNA. Liam's a good officer.

DAISY. He's a thug.

ANNA. He's a good officer. I know him.

DAISY. I've seen him incite.

ANNA. –

DAISY. Yes incite a customer.

ANNA. When?

DAISY. My first week. Two a.m. Outside a club.

ANNA. Two a.m. With a knife?

DAISY. Just two a.m. If they had a knife he wouldn't be inciting.

ANNA. He incites someone?

DAISY. YES! He starts a fight and then makes an arrest.

ANNA *shrugs*.

ANNA. You've got no pictures of you up in uniform. Nothing.

DAISY. I know. I used to. I don't know. Sometimes I have people round.

Pause.

I actually don't feel safe with him.

ANNA. Don't say that.

DAISY. He's a thug.

ANNA. Don't start a rumour.

DAISY. I'm not, he's a thug.

Pause.

Did you put in a good word for me?

ANNA. – Sure.

Pause.

DAISY. I need you to believe that what went on with my old team wasn't my fault.

ANNA. – I do.

Night.

DAISY *in pyjamas. Drinks water.*

ANNA *undoes her police belt and takes off her vest.*

ANNA. I don't feel right.

DAISY. You went all the way in to come all the way back? So they're a man down now? I bet they call me.

ANNA. I bet they don't.

Silence.

What's her name?

DAISY. I don't know. They call her something else.

ANNA. Yes.

DAISY. Gasher.

ANNA. I know her.

DAISY. No you don't.

ANNA. I think I know her.

DAISY. She's really out of it.

ANNA. I know her.

DAISY. She's my prisoner. How do you know her?

ANNA. What's she in for?

DAISY. You're the one who knows her.

ANNA. Robbing.

DAISY. Everyone's in for robbing.

ANNA. Told you.

DAISY. Anyway. We [*connected*]…

ANNA. Right.

DAISY. I've started getting through to her.

ANNA. You two chat?

DAISY. A bit.

ANNA. It's not therapy watch.

DAISY. She's talking about killing herself. So…

ANNA. She fucking won't.

DAISY. She said she might.

ANNA. I'm looking out for you now when I tell you, she won't.

DAISY. You don't know what happened.

ANNA. You're saying you're worried about her. Don't. She's manipulating you. She won't do shit. This is her shtick. I know her.

DAISY. She's a Britwell one.

ANNA. I know a gasher from there.

DAISY. It's someone else. She keeps asking for a doctor.

ANNA. Manipulative bitch.

DAISY. Even I can see there's something not right.

ANNA. It's called crack. You've got to laugh, Daisy, laugh or cry.

Pause.

DAISY. So she's sitting here and I'm sitting here. And I just watch her.

ANNA. She knows you're soft.

Is this your soft skills?

Pause.

They're very good.

DAISY. When I came into the cell she was going...

ANNA. Apeshit.

DAISY. I stepped in.

ANNA. She assault an officer? Who'd she get?

DAISY. Semi-assault. I come in and she's all quiet suddenly.

ANNA. Like a horse whisperer. You're Robert Redford.

DAISY. A bit maybe.

ANNA. What did you say to her?

DAISY. No, nothing.

ANNA. You must have said something.

DAISY. I didn't.

ANNA. Why'd she shut up?

DAISY. I don't know. I gave her some water.

ANNA. Gasher was just dehydrated.

DAISY. We talked.

ANNA. About what?

DAISY. Family.

   How it's important to both of us.

ANNA. She doesn't give a shit about your family. She'd sell her mother for a Pot Noodle.

DAISY. You don't know THIS gasher.

ANNA. I do.

DAISY. This is my gasher. I'm so tired I'm getting confused.

ANNA.…You were talking about Christmas trees and birthdays.

DAISY. I didn't think I could do heart surgery when I had a doctor boyfriend. DC Carl doesn't mean you know every-thing. We went in at the same time, Anna.

   Okay.

ANNA. I wouldn't want to be on shift with you, the way you talk at the moment.

DAISY. How do I talk?

   Pause.

ANNA. Not like the police. It was bad enough doing English with you.

   Pause.

   Did I not say well done for getting an A-star in that? Well done, Daisy. You must have NAILED *Twelfth Night*. Do you remember you complained about Mr Needham? He was a bit pervy. Harmless. 'Member?

DAISY. I haven't finished. Gasher was telling me about her family.

ANNA. She rush you?

DAISY. She was over here and I was over there. We were just talking. And at one point or another, we created this bridge.

ANNA. A bridge?

DAISY. A bridge of em-path-y.

ANNA. Whatever they told you in training. Wake up, wake up, wake up, wake up, Doris Day. Move on, move on, move on.

Pause.

DAISY. She did come at me.

ANNA. Thank you.

DAISY. She was worried about being moved away from her two kids again.

ANNA. I'm worried about you.

DAISY.…She was worried about being moved away from her two kids again.

ANNA. Then she shouldn't rob Primark.

DAISY. You do not know her.

ANNA. I do know her.

DAISY. She was worried she'd be moved and end up too far for visits.

ANNA. Poor gasher.

DAISY. Hang on…

ANNA. So she rushes you…

DAISY. I told her it wouldn't happen.

ANNA. What?

DAISY. She was there, she came towards me, and I said she wouldn't have to move away from her kids.

ANNA. Why did you say that?

DAISY. I don't know.

ANNA. What did you say?

DAISY. I said 'You won't have to move. *Necessarily.*'

ANNA. –

DAISY. *Necessarily…*

ANNA. Gasher will have to move.

DAISY. There's a possibility…

ANNA. Pack your things, gasher.

DAISY. Think about it.

ANNA. I don't need to.

DAISY. I've read about it.

ANNA. Gasher isn't Jane Eyre, Daisy.

DAISY. I know.

ANNA. Keep it simple. Don't think about it. Step one, step two, step three.

DAISY. To be a voice of 'possibility'.

ANNA. Gasher's fucked then.

DAISY. She's not fucked.

ANNA. Don't forget your toothbrush, gasher!

DAISY. I'm allowed to talk about possibility!

ANNA. No, just WATCH her.

DAISY. I can't.

ANNA. It's like TV.

DAISY. I wanted to talk to her.

ANNA. Why?

DAISY. To know I'm doing a good job.

   Pause.

   For feedback.

   Silence.

   Gasher's worried about her son.

ANNA *nods*.

She said he's got talent.

ANNA *nods*.

Music. He's good.

ANNA. Who cares.

DAISY. And now he's been done for his first assault.

ANNA. What d'you tell her?

DAISY. Asked if he'd 'Thought about the police'?

Pause.

We're both learning. Anna. We are.

ANNA. I don't think you are.

Pause.

DAISY. So she comes at me. What do I do?

Pause.

ANNA. You throw her back. Throw her against the wall. I don't
know if I can actually advise you any more because you
don't even seem connected with the team. Where's your
fucking empathy bridge with your team? You need them to
BACK you.

DAISY. Come on, they're scum.

ANNA. Shut up.

DAISY. They are scum.

I wish I could say they were racist against me. The R-word
has got something to it at least. Some currency. I wish I
could say something about it that would mean something,
but there's nothing everyone can't handle. Can't get on with.

ANNA. Shut up.

DAISY. You've just stopped noticing how they treat us. My old
team, this team, any team – scummy people.

ANNA. Here's some feedback – it's not US, Daisy. You got a
fucking transfer. Think about what that says. You make the
kind of complaints that have the rest of us living like 'pigs'.
You haven't even given this team a chance. It's you, Daisy,
take some fucking responsibility. You depress me. You make
people think women, like me, who have tried fucking hard,
shouldn't be in the force.

DAISY. You should back me. You should thank me for taking
the hit. You should say 'Thank you Daisy.'

ANNA *spits in her face*.

ANNA. Thank you.

Come on.

DAISY *moves away*.

ANNA *kicks out at her so she trips*.

I'm allowed to do that.

Sexism is so ism-lite. You can use it as your 'ism' at interview as an example of a personal situation. Your 'path-to-
promotion narrative' of how you have dealt with challenging
situations in a modern workplace. It's ideal. I find you slow. I
know you and I find you slow. You're not as good as them.

DAISY. I'm disempowered.

ANNA. FUCK. OFF.

DAISY. All of the 'shag me – I'm not going out on shift with a
bird – posh bitch – too thin – cock-tease – instinctively feel
you're not as good but can't examine why – she's a slag'
shit. Chip, chip, chip, chip. I did the right thing.

You dismiss women too. You think you don't because you're
a woman, but you're a product of the same old shit. You
don't trust them.

ANNA. Remember when they said the force was insti, institu-
tionally racist. So everyone watched what they said for the
FEAR of GOD of being called a racist, of having that on
your record. Now they say, calling the force racist stops the

force performing properly, so now they've done a review and called the force not racist.

DAISY. I don't know. Yes.

ANNA. What do we call Abdul?

DAISY. 'Brown.'

ANNA. 'Hey Brown, how are you?' 'See you later Brown'. It's not the force. It's people.

DAISY. But this is my WORK. This is the POLICE. They're lucky to have graduates like us. I could have been anything.

She cries.

ANNA. Yes, you were going to be an inventor. Or run the UN.

DAISY. I could be the best fucking police officer they ever had. As soon as I get off the beat.

ANNA. You don't know what the word police officer means. This is the test. He who survives, wins.

DAISY *waits for* ANNA *to comfort her. She doesn't.* DAISY *gradually composes herself.*

Silence.

Carl called me.

DAISY. –

ANNA. I can stay somewhere else.

DAISY. Have you even seen him since you fell out?

ANNA. At work.

DAISY. I meant outside of work.

ANNA. What 'outside of work'?

I can just as easy stay with someone else on the team.

DAISY. No don't.

Silence.

ANNA. He's talking.

DAISY. What's he saying?

ANNA. He loves me.

DAISY. DC Carl loves PC Anna.

ANNA. He said he loves me.

DAISY. Then that's nice.

After a night out.

DAISY. I shouldn't have used my pass for the Tube.

ANNA. Fuck it.

DAISY. No. I feel shit.

ANNA. Doesn't matter.

DAISY. Does matter.

ANNA. Nothing happened.

DAISY. If there was a fight.

ANNA. We'd have piled in.

DAISY. If you travel free, you're, it's like you're on duty.

ANNA. We usually are on duty. I liked that place.

DAISY. I would have had to do something.

ANNA. I would have got off. Gone to another club. Let them
kill each other.

DAISY. I would have stopped it, the fight or whatever. 'Stop,
police!'

Silence.

Can't face going back to cell watch tomorrow.

ANNA. A job, isn't it.

DAISY. Our job.

ANNA. Actually I've seen Carl use his pass when he was pissed.

Pause.

And he's what I would call a 'Good Officer'.

DAISY. Would you?

ANNA. Yes. A good fucking officer.

Pause.

DAISY. What would he do with gasher?

ANNA. Gasher?

DAISY. My gasher.

ANNA. With your gasher?

DAISY. My gasher?

ANNA. If she rushed him?

DAISY. Yeah? What would Carl do?

ANNA. Snap her in half.

DAISY. I'm worrying about tomorrow now.

ANNA. Just do your time on cell watch. Then I can say some good Daisy-type-stuff about you.

DAISY. You said you already did.

ANNA. If she bullshits you...

DAISY. I know.

ANNA. She wants water. Get water.

DAISY. I know.

ANNA. She wants a doctor. Get a doctor.

DAISY. I know.

ANNA. She wants her kids. Tough shit.

Pause.

DAISY. They all ask for a doctor.

ANNA. Yes.

DAISY. Doctor, doctor.

ANNA. Yes.

DAISY. Tough shit.

ANNA. You have to get a doctor.

Pause.

DAISY. You have to get them a doctor.

Pause.

ANNA. Don't worry, you can sort it tomorrow.

Pause.

DAISY. Tomorrow I'll be a good officer. I do want to be a good
officer. That's why I wanted to do this in the first place. I just
need to learn to 'Keep it simple'.

I'll get gasher a doctor, I'll throw gasher against the wall and
– tell me the right words to say and I'll say it. What should I
say?

ANNA. Talk to the team.

Pause.

He butted me.

DAISY. Okay.

ANNA. That's what got my lip.

DAISY. I thought maybe.

ANNA. Oh.

Pause.

I didn't get mugged.

DAISY. That's good.

ANNA. It's good I didn't get mugged.

DAISY. Carl whacked you one?

ANNA. I shouldn't have said.

DAISY. It's okay. I thought maybe.

ANNA. You knew it did you?

DAISY. All I see is DV.

ANNA. Me too.

DAISY. DV, DV, DV.

ANNA. Me too.

DAISY. Experts.

Pause.

What do you want to do?

ANNA. Like what?

DAISY. I don't know.

ANNA. I should talk to him.

Silence.

I can't talk to him. I have to work with him.

DAISY. You don't HAVE to work with him.

ANNA. You think I should say something?

DAISY. I don't know. You have that option, don't you, to say something. You know all the options. And then, well then it's said isn't it.

Silence.

I want it to be okay with this team, you know, now that I'm here. And I feel sort of involved. Because you're staying here. Whatever you chose to do. It affects me as well. I'm just putting that out there. As a thing.

Silence.

In a way, he's made it a bit easier for you.

ANNA. 'Easier'?

DAISY. In the team?

ANNA. He hit me.

DAISY. But a DC on your side, I mean. DC Carl. In the MET. On your side. You've been MAST-trained, you haven't had the same sort of trouble. He makes it easier. I'm just saying, from where I stand… in my experience.

Pause.

I could use a Carl, in a way!

ANNA. In a weird way.

DAISY. Oh yeah, in a weird way.

ANNA *starts to cry.*

It's those pills…

Pause.

Should be illegal.

ANNA *looks at her.*

You've made me feel this team might be okay. Thank you.

ANNA. And thanks for not saying anything.

DAISY. I won't say or do anything.

Silence.

ANNA. Is there any Night Nurse left?

DAISY. No.

The End.

A Nick Hern Book

Charged first published in Great Britain in 2010 as a paperback original by Nick Hern Books Limited, 14 Larden Road, London W3 7ST, in association with Clean Break

Reprinted in this revised edition in 2011

Cover design: Ned Hoste, 2H
Cover image: plainpicture/Westend61

Typeset by Nick Hern Books, London
Printed and bound in Great Britain by CLE Print Ltd, St Ives, Cambs, PE27 3LE

A CIP catalogue record for this book is available from the British Library

ISBN 978 1 84842 129 5

FSC
www.fsc.org
MIX
From responsible sources
FSC® C019549